At Issue

Do Abstinence
Programs Work?

Other Books in the At Issue Series:

At Issue

Do Abstinence Programs Work?

Christine Watkins, Book Editor

GREENHAVEN PRESS
A part of Gale, Cengage Learning

GALE
CENGAGE Learning

Farmington Hills, Mich • San Francisco • New York • Waterville, Maine
Meriden, Conn • Mason, Ohio • Chicago

Elizabeth Des Chenes, *Director, Content Strategy*
Douglas Dentino, *Manager, New Product*

© 2014 Greenhaven Press, a part of Gale, Cengage Learning.

WCN: 01-100-101

Gale and Greenhaven Press are registered trademarks used herein under license.

For more information, contact:
Greenhaven Press
27500 Drake Rd.
Farmington Hills, MI 48331-3535
Or you can visit our Internet site at gale.cengage.com

For product information and technology assistance, contact us at

Gale Customer Support, 1-800-877-4253
For permission to use material from this text or product, submit all requests online at
www.cengage.com/permissions

Further permissions questions can be e-mailed to permissionrequest@cengage.com

Articles in Greenhaven Press anthologies are often edited for length to meet page require-ments. In addition, original titles of these works are changed to clearly present the main thesis and to explicitly indicate the author's opinion. Every effort is made to ensure that Greenhaven Press accurately reflects the original intent of the authors. Every effort has been made to trace the owners of copyrighted material.

Cover image © Images.com/Corbis.

LIBRARY OF CONGRESS CATALOGING-IN-PUBLICATION DATA

Do abstinence programs work? / Christine Watkins, book editor.
    pages cm. -- (At issue)
    Includes bibliographical references and index.
    ISBN 978-0-7377-6828-2 (hardcover) -- ISBN 978-0-7377-6829-9 (pbk.)
    1. Teenagers--Sexual behavior--United States. 2. Sexual abstinence--United States. 3. Sex instruction for teenagers--United States. 4. Pregnancy, Unwanted--United States. I. Watkins, Christine, 1951-
    HQ800.15.D62 2014
    306.70835--dc23
                                                                2013050904

Printed in the United States of America
1 2 3 4 5 6 7 18 17 16 15 14

Contents

Introduction

Sex education in the United States goes back to the late nineteenth century and early twentieth century when Americans began to move from farms and rural areas into cities. In 1892, the National Education Association (NEA) called for "moral education in the schools," and in 1912 it recommended that teachers learn how to instruct children about sex. In 1913, Chicago became the first major city to incorporate an actual sex education program in high schools. This early sex education reflected the Victorian values of the time, such as the notion that sexually transmitted diseases (STDs) were a punishment for immoral behavior. A sex education film of the 1920s produced by the American Social Hygiene Association, *The Gift of Life*, warned students that masturbation—the "solitary vice"—could "hinder a boy's progress towards vigorous manhood," and in 1920 an English teacher named Lucy S. Curtiss wrote in an article titled "Sex Instruction Through English Literature" that sexual activity was "the sin of yielding to impure desire."

The federal government first became involved in sex education out of concern over the spread of STDs among soldiers during World War I, and in 1918 allocated funding to instruct soldiers about syphilis, gonorrhea, and sexual hygiene. Over the next three decades, sex education continued to expand with the US Office of Education, the US Public Health Service, and the NEA publishing materials and training teachers. In 1968, the US Office of Education funded New York University to develop graduate programs for training sex education teachers.

Beginning in the 1960s, however, public opposition to sex education in schools began to assert itself. Opponents organized their dissent into claims that sex education attacked traditional moral values, promoted promiscuity among young people, and infringed on parental authority. In school districts throughout the United States, parents started protesting against sex education programs. But with the onset of the AIDS and HIV pandemic in the 1980s, US Surgeon General C. Everett Koop called for sex education—including information on safe sex and HIV prevention—to be instituted in all public schools, and by the mid-1990s every state had passed some form of sex education mandate. Opponents of sex education had little choice but to acquiesce; however, instead of giving up completely, they formulated a different approach: acknowledge the importance of sex education but emphasize the message that sexual activity before marriage has severe physical and emotional consequences and should be discouraged. In other words, transform sex education to "abstinence education."

Proponents of abstinence education believe that comprehensive sex education encourages premarital sexual activity among teenagers and consider the epidemic of STDs and the widespread problem of teenage pregnancy to be the result. Maintaining that teaching abstinence in schools is the only viable solution, they convinced school boards and national politicians throughout the 1980s and early 1990s to develop and adopt abstinence-only-until-marriage sex education programs. Federal funding for such programs began in 1982 with the passage of the Adolescent Family Life Act (AFLA), and it increased dramatically in 1996 with enactment of Title V of the Social Security Act. This legislation allocated fifty million dollars a year to states with abstinence-only sex education curricula, provided the programs followed an eight-point definition, often referred to as "A-H." The government's funding for abstinence education continued to grow until it reached more than one billion dollars in total. According to the US Social Security Act, Section 510(b)(2), the eight-point definition of an abstinence education program is one that:

(A) Has as its exclusive purpose, teaching the social, psychological, and health gains to be realized by abstaining from sexual activity;

(B) Teaches abstinence from sexual activity outside marriage as the expected standard for all school-age children;

(C) Teaches that abstinence from sexual activity is the only certain way to avoid out-of-wedlock pregnancy, sexually transmitted diseases, and other associated health problems;

(D) Teaches that a mutually faithful monogamous relationship in the context of marriage is the expected standard of human sexual activity;

(E) Teaches that sexual activity outside the context of marriage is likely to have harmful psychological and physical effects;

(F) Teaches that bearing children out-of-wedlock is likely to have harmful consequences for the child, the child's parents, and society;

(G) Teaches young people how to reject sexual advances and how alcohol and drug use increase vulnerability to sexual advances; and

(H) Teaches the importance of attaining self-sufficiency before engaging in sexual activity.

Opponents and critics of abstinence education, which include medical and adolescent health professionals, have not remained silent and argue that such programs do not decrease the likelihood that teenagers will have sex. In fact, the Centers for Disease Control and Prevention (CDC) reported that as of 2011, 47.4 percent of high school students have had sexual intercourse. And according to the Guttmacher Institute, a third of teens aged fifteen to seventeen have had no formal education on contraceptives, and approximately 9.1 million fifteen- to twenty-four-year-olds contract sexually transmitted infections every year. Furthermore, the Society for Adolescent Medicine reported in the 2006 *Journal of Adolescent Health* that "current federal abstinence-only-until-marriage policy is ethically problematic, as it excludes accurate information about contraception, misinforms by overemphasizing or misstating the risks of contraception, and fails to require the use of scientifically accurate information while promoting approaches of questionable value."

The US debate concerning the most appropriate type of sex education for school-age youth—abstinence or comprehensive—continues to rage with no indication of subsiding. One thing has remained consistent, however, and that is the public support for sex education in general. According to the Future of Sex Education, an organization that promotes comprehensive sex education in schools, national polls reveal 93 percent of Americans support "sex or sexuality courses being taught" in high school and 84 percent support such instruction in junior high. The authors included in *At Issue: Do Abstinence Programs Work?* present a variety of opinions surrounding the subject of abstinence sex education, including its effect on teen pregnancy and sexually transmitted diseases, federal funding of sex education programs, and what topics should be included in the curriculum.

1

Abstinence Education Programs Are Effective

Christine Kim and Robert Rector

Christine Kim is a policy analyst and Robert Rector is a senior research fellow in the domestic policy studies department at the Heritage Foundation, a research and educational institution.

Teens who engage in sexual activity put themselves at risk for many negative outcomes, including sexually transmitted infections, lower academic achievement, pregnancy, and reduced overall well-being. It is, therefore, vitally important for children to receive abstinence education to learn the consequences of early sexual activity, valuable life and decision-making skills, and the benefits of developing healthy relationships. Furthermore, studies have shown that abstinence education programs are effective in delaying sexual initiation, reducing early sexual activity, and decreasing the number of sexual partners among adolescents.

Teen sexual activity remains a widespread problem confronting the nation. Each year, some 2.6 million teenagers become sexually active—a rate of 7,000 teens per day. Among high school students, nearly half report having engaged in sexual activity, and one-third are currently active.

Abstinence Protects Youth

Sexual activity during teenage years poses serious health risks for youths and has long-term implications. Early sexual activity is associated with an increased risk of sexually transmitted diseases (STDs), reduced psychological and emotional well-being, lower academic achievement, teen pregnancy, and out-of-wedlock childbearing. Many of these risks are avoidable if teens choose to abstain from sexual activity. Abstinence is the surest way to avoid the risk of STDs and unwed childbearing.

Abstinence education "teaches abstinence from sexual activity outside marriage as the expected standard for all school age children" and stresses the social, psychological, and health benefits of abstinence. Abstinence programs also provide youths with valuable life and decision-making skills that lay the foundation for personal responsibility and developing healthy relationships and marriages later in life. These programs emphasize preparing young people for future-oriented goals.

Studies have shown that abstinent teens report, on average, better psychological well-being and higher educational attainment than those who are sexually active. Delaying the initiation of or reducing early sexual activity among teens can decrease their overall exposure to risks of unwed childbearing, STDs, and psycho-emotional harm. Authentic abstinence programs are therefore crucial to efforts aimed at reducing unwed childbearing and improving youth well-being. . . .

Studies That Reported Positive Behavioral Change

Abstinence-only Intervention. A 2010 study in the medical journal *Archives of Pediatrics and Adolescent Medicine*, published by the American Medical Association, concludes that an "abstinence-only intervention reduced sexual initiation" as well as recent sexual activity among a group of African-American adolescents. Two years after attending an eight-hour abstinence program, about one-third of the participants had initiated sexual activity, compared to nearly one-half of the non-participants who enrolled in a general health program. That is, the abstinence program reduced the rate of sexual initiation by one-third. Moreover, abstinence program participants who became sexually active were not less likely to use contraception.

By contrast, the study also evaluated two alternative interventions, one that only taught contraception (i.e., the "safe sex" approach) and another that contained both abstinence and contraception content (i.e., comprehensive sex education), and found that neither program delayed or reduced teen sexual activity. Furthermore, these programs, whose main emphasis is on contraception, failed to increase use among adolescents. . . .

Reasons of the Heart. Taught over 20 class periods by certified and program-trained health educators, the Reasons of the Heart (ROH) curriculum focuses on individual character development and teaches adolescents the benefits that are associated with abstinence until marriage.

Researchers found that . . . upper-elementary students who participated in [the] Sex Can Wait [program] were less likely than non-participants to report engaging in recent sexual activity.

A 2008 study evaluated the ROH curriculum's impact on adolescent sexual activity among seventh grade students in three suburban northern Virginia public schools. The researchers also collected data on a comparison group of seventh grade students in two nearby middle schools that did not participate in the program. Students in those schools instead received the state's standard family life education, which included two videos on HIV/ STD prevention and one on abstinence.

The evaluators surveyed seventh grade students in all five schools before and after the program. They found that, a year after the program, 32 (9.2 percent) of the 347 ROH students who were virgins at the initial survey had initiated sexual activity, compared with 31 (or 16.4 percent) of the 189 comparison group students. Controlling for the differences between the comparison group and ROH students, the study reported that ROH students were half as likely as comparison group students to initiate sexual activity. The evaluators concluded, "This result appears to compare favorably to the reductions in initiation achieved by some of the abstinence programs [evaluated in earlier studies]."

Sex Can Wait. Sex Can Wait is a three-series abstinence education program with one series for upper-elementary students, a second for middle school students, and a third for high school students. The Sex Can Wait program lasts five weeks and offers lessons on character building, important life skills, and reproductive biology. . . .

The researchers found that, 18 months after the program, upper-elementary students who participated in Sex Can Wait were less likely than non-participants to report engaging in recent sexual activity. Among middle school students, participants were also less likely than non-participants to report engaging in sexual activity ever and in the preceding month before the 18-month follow-up. Finally, among high school students, the authors found reduced levels of sexual activity in the short term but not in the 18-month follow-up.

Heritage Keepers. Heritage Keepers is a primary prevention abstinence program for middle school and high school students. The program offers an interactive three-year, two-level curriculum.

To assess Heritage Keepers' impact, a group of evaluators compared some 1,200 virgin students who attended schools that faithfully implemented the program to some 250 students in demographically and geographically comparable schools who did not receive the abstinence intervention. One year after the program, 14.5 percent of Heritage Keepers students had become sexually active compared with 26.5 percent of the comparison group.

Overall, Heritage Keepers students "were about one-half as likely" as comparison group students to initiate sex after adjusting for pre-program differences between the two groups. The study found similar results in subsets of African-American students, Caucasian students, boys, and girls.

For Keeps. A study published in 2005 evaluated the For Keeps curriculum as implemented in five urban and two suburban middle schools in the Midwest. Schools were assigned by the school districts to receive the program, which was part of a county-wide teen pregnancy prevention initiative.

Taught by outside facilitators, For Keeps was a five-day curriculum with 40-minute sessions that focused on character development and the benefits of abstinence and tried to help students understand how pregnancy and sexually transmitted diseases can impede their long-term goals. It also emphasized the psycho-emotional and economic consequences of early sexual activity. The curriculum was intended both for students who had become sexually active and for those who had not.

A 2005 study evaluated the District of Columbia's Best Friends program ... [and found] that Best Friends girls were nearly 6.5 times more likely to abstain from sexual activity than [non-participant] respondents.

The evaluation collected data on all students through a pretest survey, and some 2,000 youths (about 70 percent of those who took the pretest survey) responded to a follow-up survey conducted about five months after the program ended. Among youths who engaged in any sexual behavior during the follow-up period, some who participated in For Keeps reported a reduction in "the amount of casual sex, as evidenced by fewer episodes of sex and fewer sexual partners" during the evaluation period, although program participants did not differ from non-participants in the likelihood of engaging in sexual activity during the follow-up interval.

Best Friends. The Best Friends (BF) program began in 1987 and operates in about 90 schools across the United States. The Best Friends curriculum is an abstinence-based character-building program for girls starting in the sixth grade and offers a variety of services such as group discussions, mentoring, and community activities. Discussion topics include friendship, love and dating, self-respect, decision making, alcohol and drug abuse, physical fitness and nutrition, and AIDS/STDs. The curriculum's predominant theme is encouraging youths to abstain from high-risk behaviors and sexual activity.

A 2005 study evaluated the District of Columbia's Best Friends program, which operated in six of the District's 20 middle schools. The study compared data on BF participants to data from the Youth Risk Behavior Surveys (YRBS) conducted for the District. When the authors of the study compared Best Friends schools to District schools that did not have the program, they found that Best Friends schools tended to be located in the more disadvantaged sections of the city and were academically comparable to or slightly worse than the District's middle schools in general.

Adjusting for the survey year, students' age, grade, and race and ethnicity, the study reported that Best Friends girls were nearly 6.5 times more likely to abstain from sexual activity than YRBS respondents. They were 2.4 times more likely to abstain from smoking, 8.1 times more likely to abstain from illegal drug use, and 1.9 times more likely to abstain from drinking.

Not Me, Not Now. Not Me, Not Now, a community-wide abstinence intervention program, targeted children ages nine through 14 in Monroe County, New York, which includes the city of Rochester. The Not Me, Not Now program devised a mass communications strategy to promote the abstinence message through paid television and radio advertising, billboards, posters distributed in schools, educational materials for parents, an interactive Web site, and educational sessions in school and community settings. The program had five objectives: raising awareness of the problem of teen pregnancy, increasing understanding of the negative consequences of teen pregnancy, developing resistance to peer pressure, promoting parent-child communication, and promoting abstinence among teens.

Not Me, Not Now was effective in reaching early teens, with some 95 percent of the target audience in the county reporting that they had seen a Not Me, Not Now ad. During the intervention period, there was a statistically significant positive shift in attitudes among pre-teens and early teens in the county.

The sexual activity rate of 15-year-olds across the county dropped by a statistically significant amount, from 46.6 percent to 31.6 percent, during this period. The pregnancy rate for girls ages 15 through 17 in Monroe County fell by a statistically significant amount, from 63.4 pregnancies per 1,000 girls to 49.5 pregnancies per 1,000. The teen pregnancy rate fell more rapidly in Monroe County than in comparison counties and upstate New York in general, and the differences in the rates of decrease were statistically significant.

Youths who had engaged in prior sexual activity and participated in the stand-alone Stay SMART program exhibited reduced levels of recent sexual activity compared with non-participants.

Abstinence by Choice. Abstinence by Choice operated in 20 schools in the Little Rock area of Arkansas. The program targeted seventh, eighth, and ninth grade students and reached about 4,000 youths each year. The curriculum included a five-day workshop with speakers, presentations, skits, videos, and an adult mentoring component.

A 2001 evaluation analyzed a sample of 329 students and found that only 5.9 percent of eighth grade girls who had participated in Abstinence by Choice a year earlier had initiated sexual activity compared with 10.2 percent of non-participants. Among eighth grade boy participants, 15.8 percent had initiated sexual activity, compared with 22.8 percent among non-participating boys. (The sexual activity rate of students in the program was compared with the rate of sexual activity among control students in the same grade and schools prior to commencement of the program.). . .

Stay SMART. Delivered to Boys and Girls Clubs of America participants, Stay SMART integrated abstinence education with substance-use prevention and incorporated instructions on general life skills as well. The 12-session curriculum, led by Boys and Girls Club staff, used a postponement approach to early sexual activity and targeted both sexually experienced and sexually inexperienced adolescents. Participation in Boys and Girls Clubs and Stay SMART was voluntary. . . .

The study found that, two years after the program, youths who had engaged in prior sexual activity and participated in the stand-alone Stay SMART program exhibited reduced levels of recent sexual activity compared with non-participants and, interestingly, participants in the Stay SMART-plus-boosters program as well. Among participants who were virgins prior to the program, the study did not find a statistically significant program effect.

An evaluation of the Teen Aid and Sex Respect abstinence programs in three Utah school districts reported that certain groups of youths who received these programs delayed the initiation of sexual activity.

Project Taking Charge. Project Taking Charge was a six-week abstinence curriculum delivered in home economics classes during the school year. It was designed for use in low-income communities with high rates of teen pregnancy. The curriculum contained elements on self-development; basic information about sexual biology (e.g., anatomy, physiology, and pregnancy); vocational goal-setting; family communication; and values instruction on the importance of delaying sexual activity until marriage.

The program was evaluated in Wilmington, Delaware, and West Point, Mississippi, based on a small sample of 91 adolescents. Control and experimental groups were created by randomly assigning classrooms either to receive or not to receive the program. The students were assessed immediately before and after the program and at a six-month follow-up. In the six-month follow-up, Project Taking Charge was shown to have had a statistically significant effect in increasing adolescents' knowledge of the problems associated with teen pregnancy, the problems of sexually transmitted diseases, and reproductive biology.

The program may also have delayed the onset of sexual activity among some of the participants. About 23 percent of participants who were virgins at the pretest initiated sexual activity during the follow-up interval, compared with 50 percent of the youths in the control group, although the authors urged caution in interpreting these numbers due to the small sample size.

Teen Aid and Sex Respect. An evaluation of the Teen Aid and Sex Respect abstinence programs in three Utah school districts reported that certain groups of youths who received these programs delayed the initiation of sexual activity. To determine the effects of the programs, students in schools with the abstinence programs were compared with students in similar control schools within the same school districts. Statistical adjustments were applied to control for any initial differences between program participants and control group students.

In the aggregate sample, the researchers did not find any differences in the rates of sexual initiation between youths who had received abstinence education and those who had not. However, analyzing a cohort of high school students who had fairly permissive attitudes, they found that program participants were one-third less likely to engage in sexual activity one year after the programs compared with non-participants (22.4 percent versus 37 percent).

Although 80 percent of parents want schools to teach youths to abstain from sexual activity until they are in a committed adult romantic relationship nearing marriage . . . these parental values are rarely communicated in the classroom.

Even when the researchers adjusted for students' dating and drinking behavior, religious involvement, family composition, peer pressure, and other factors, the differences between the two groups remained statistically significant. (Statistically significant changes in behavior were not found among a similar group of junior high school students.) The researchers found it notable that youths who had more permissive attitudes were "not only receptive and responsive to the abstinence message in the short run, but that some influence on behavior [was] also occurring." . . .

Abstinence Programs Benefit Society

Although 80 percent of parents want schools to teach youths to abstain from sexual activity until they are in a committed adult romantic relationship nearing marriage—the core message of abstinence education—these parental values are rarely communicated in the classroom.

In the classroom, the prevailing mentality often condones teen sexual activity as long as youths use contraceptives. Abstinence is usually mentioned only in passing, if at all. Sadly, many teens who need to learn about the benefits of abstaining from sexual activity during the teenage years never hear them, and many students who choose to abstain fail to receive adequate support for their decisions.

Teen sexual activity is costly, not just for teens, but also for society. Teens who engage in sexual activity risk a host of negative outcomes including STD infection, emotional and psychological harm, lower educational attainment, and out-of-wedlock childbearing.

Genuine abstinence education is therefore crucial to the physical and psycho-emotional well-being of the nation's youth. In addition to teaching the benefits of abstaining from sexual activity until marriage, abstinence programs focus on developing character traits that prepare youths for future-oriented goals.

When considering effective prevention programs aimed at changing teen sexual behavior, lawmakers should consider *all* of the available empirical evidence and restore funding for abstinence education.

2

Abstinence Education Programs Are Not Effective

The Healthy Colorado Youth Alliance and the Sexuality Information and Education Council of the United States

The Healthy Colorado Youth Alliance advocates for comprehensive sex education throughout Colorado by informing public policy and organizing communities. The Sexuality Information and Education Council of the United States is a clearinghouse for information on sexuality, with a special interest in sex education.

Abstinence-only sex education programs rely on fear- and shame-based messages that disparage any sexual activity outside of marriage as well as the use of condoms and contraception. Numerous studies have proven that these programs are not effective; they do not delay initiation of sexual activity, reduce the number of sexual partners, or reduce the teen pregnancy rate. Yet individual states continue to receive federal funding for teaching abstinence programs in schools. The reality is school-aged children are having sex and need medically accurate information about how to reduce their risk of unintended pregnancy and sexually transmitted infections, information that abstinence programs do not provide.

Beginning in 1981 under the administration of President Ronald Reagan, the federal government increasingly put its support and money behind abstinence-only-until-marriage programs. By the year 2000 there existed three separate funding streams supporting these programs—the *Adolescent Family Life Act* (AFLA), the Title V abstinence-only-until-marriage program, and the Community-Based Abstinence Education (CBAE) grant program. Over the past three decades, the federal government has invested heavily in these programs, spending more than $1.5 billion on them. Funding for these unproven programs grew exponentially between 1996 and 2008, particularly during the years of the George W. Bush administration, despite an overwhelming body of research proving them to be ineffective at achieving their stated goals.

Abstinence Education Programs Are Out of Touch with Reality

Along with these funding streams the federal government developed an eight-point definition of "abstinence education." Among other things, this definition requires programs to teach that "a mutually faithful monogamous relationship in the context of marriage is the expected standard of sexual activity" and that "sexual activity outside of the context of marriage is likely to have harmful psychological and physical effects." Organizations using federal abstinence-only-until-marriage funds must comply with this federal definition. Despite this focus on marriage, the reality is that research from 2009 shows that 46% of all high-school-aged students in the United States have already had sex. These adolescents need information about how to protect themselves from unintended pregnancy, HIV, and other sexually transmitted infections (STIs) before they are sexually active. Even of those who are able to marry, fewer than 7% of men and 20% of women 18 to 50 years old were virgins when they were married, and only 10% of adult men and 22% of adult women report their first sexual intercourse was with their spouse. Today, there are more than 87 million American adults who are classified as single because they have either delayed marriage, decided to remain single, divorced, or entered into gay or lesbian partnerships. It is not reasonable to expect these adults to adhere to this "standard," nor is it accurate to teach young people that all adults do adhere to it.

Abstinence-only-until-marriage programs are required to promote ideas that are scientifically questionable and withhold public health and lifesaving information.

Research Proves Abstinence Programs Are Not Beneficial

There is clear evidence that abstinence-only-until-marriage programs are not effective in stopping or even delaying teen sexual activity. Since the federal government began funding single-purpose abstinence-only-until-marriage promotion programs in the 1980s, an overwhelming body of research has developed proving these programs to be utterly ineffective. For example, a 2007 study on behalf of the Department of Health and Human Services, conducted by Mathematica Policy Research over nine years and at a cost of almost $8 million, closely examined four programs supported by Title V abstinence-only-until-marriage dollars. Out of 700 programs, the four programs studied weren't selected randomly—they were handpicked because they were thought to be the most promising abstinence-only-until-marriage programs being funded by the government. After following more than 2,000 teens for as long as six years, the evaluation found that none of the four programs was able to demonstrate a statistically significant beneficial impact on young people's sexual behavior. Individuals who participated in the programs were no more likely to abstain than those who did not. As prominent researcher Dr. Doug Kirby has noted, "This was a very rigorous study with very clear results."

That same year, the National Campaign to Prevent Teen and Unplanned Pregnancy released *Emerging Answers 2007*, an authoritative and comprehensive review of research findings on the effectiveness of HIV and sex education programs. The report concludes that despite improvements in the quality and quantity of evaluation research in this field "there does not exist any strong evidence that any abstinence program delays the initiation of sex, hastens the return to abstinence, or reduces the number of sexual partners."

Abstinence-only-until-marriage programs have also been sharply criticized by leading medical professional organizations for being, by their very nature, antithetical to the principles of science and medical ethics. As a matter of federal law, abstinence-only-until-marriage programs are required to promote ideas that are scientifically questionable and withhold public health and lifesaving information, such as a full discussion of how to use condoms as protection from HIV transmission. As such, they may not credibly assert that they are "medically accurate." It is little wonder, then, that leading health professional organizations—including the American Medical Association, the American Academy of Pediatrics, the Society of Adolescent Medicine, and the American Psychological Association—have raised serious ethical concerns about the government's support for such programs. . . .

Every major medical and public health organization in this country and around the globe agrees that abstinence-only-until-marriage programs are not best for young people.

While AFLA and the CBAE programs were actively eliminated by Congress, the Title V abstinence-only-until-marriage program was allowed to expire. This program was originally authorized for five years, 1998–2002. After years of continuing resolutions extending the program, it was officially reauthorized in July 2008 for a 12-month extension. When that year was up on June 30, 2009, Congress deliberately took no action, thereby allowing the program to expire. At the time of its expiration in June 2009, nearly half the states, including Colorado, had rejected funding for this unsuccessful program. Of the states that refused the money at the time of the program's end, over 80 percent did so based on the strong research and evaluations showing that abstinence-only-until-marriage efforts are ineffective. However, after its expiration, multiple attempts were made by conservative members of Congress to revive the program, and they were ultimately successful. In late fall of 2009, conservatives in Congress led by Senator Orrin Hatch (R-UT), managed to insert funding for the Title V abstinence-only-until-marriage program in Senate health care reform legislation (the *Patient Protection and Affordable Care Act*) and the language remained in the final legislation signed by President [Barack] Obama. This extension equals another $250 million for failed abstinence-only-until-marriage programs over the next five years (2010–2014). The Title V abstinence-only-until-marriage program continues to require states to provide an expensive match of three state dollars for every four federal dollars received, including in-kind matches.

Comprehensive Sex Education Is the Better Choice

The Title V abstinence-only-until-marriage program should never have been resurrected, particularly as part of the most ambitious and progressive social legislation in decades, and in a time when most young people have sex for the first time at about age 17 but do not marry until their middle or late 20s, leaving young adults at risk of unintended pregnancies, STIs, and HIV for nearly a decade. It was never about public health or even about pregnancy prevention—the creators of the program were clear, it "was intended to align Congress with the social tradition . . . that sex should be confined to married couples"—and Colorado needs to ensure that these ideologically driven funds do not come back into the state.

Every major medical and public health organization in this country and around the globe agrees that abstinence-only-until-marriage programs are not best for young people. Instead, following the evidence of what works, they believe in the importance of providing comprehensive sexuality education. Beginning in 2009, the federal government finally began heeding the evidence and the urgings of the nation's leading medical and public health organizations, parents, and advocates, and dedicated funding for more comprehensive approaches to sex education through two separate funding streams—the President's Teen Pregnancy Prevention Initiative and the Personal Responsibility Education Program—totaling nearly $190 million.

The promotion of one set of social values based on religious belief is not appropriate in a public school setting.

With the advent of the Obama administration, new federal funding streams supporting more comprehensive approaches to sex education have also been created. Along with eliminating CBAE and AFLA funding for abstinence-only-until-marriage programs, the *Consolidated Appropriations Act of 2010* dedicated $114.5 million to a new grant program, the President's Teen Pregnancy Prevention Initiative. The new initiative grants funding directly to public and private entities to implement medically accurate and age-appropriate evidence-based programs or innovative approaches that will effectively "reduce teenage pregnancy [and] behavioral risk factors underlying teenage pregnancy."

While recent health care reform legislation, the *Patient Protection and Affordable Care Act*, included an extension of the failed Title V abstinence-only-until-marriage program, it also created the Personal Responsibility Education Program (PREP), which will offer individual states grants for comprehensive sex education programs that provide young people with complete, medically accurate, and age-appropriate sex education in order to help them reduce their risk of unintended pregnancy, HIV/AIDS, and other STIs. Programs funded by PREP are also required to foster the development of life skills so that young people can make informed decisions and lead safe and healthy lives. The program totals $75 million per year in mandatory funding for Fiscal Years 2010–2014. Drafters of the legislation were careful to define key terms in the legislation—such as "age appropriate" and "medically accurate and complete"—with the hope that programs funded under this legislation would not fall prey to the same misinformation and misuse of taxpayer dollars as federally funded abstinence-only-until-marriage programs. PREP also includes much-needed funding dedicated to tribes and tribal organizations, research and evaluation, and innovative approaches; it is the first-ever dedicated funding stream for comprehensive sex education, and will support efforts by states to provide their young people with real sex education. . . .

Abstinence Education Curricula Can Harm Young People

In an effort to raise awareness on the issue, this report aims to inform local advocates, community members, parents, youth, and school administrators of the ineffective programs provided to young people by the state's prominent abstinence-only-until-marriage program providers. Through information gathered from the four CBAE-funded organizations and annual reports obtained through a Freedom of Information Act request, as well as additional on-the-ground research, this report provides an in-depth look at the program and curricula used by these organizations, their partnerships with other ultraconservative groups, and the communities, school districts, and populations they target. What is made clear by the report is that these organizations promulgate an extreme religious, conservative, and ideologically driven agenda through their abstinence-only-until-marriage programs. These programs do not provide young people with full and complete sexual health information—nor are they intended to do so—but instead aim to promote one specific set of social values. These ideologically held beliefs honor the sanctity of marriage to the exclusion of diverse unions and family formations. The promotion of one set of social values based on religious belief is not appropriate in a public school setting—where many of these programs are administered. In addition, messages contained in abstinence-only-until-marriage programs typically rely on fear- and shame-based messages to convince young people to remain abstinent. These messages condemn sexual activity outside of marriage and disparage the use of condoms and contraception. Such instruction is harmful to young people and contradicts public health knowledge of effective prevention methods for unintended pregnancy and STIs. These abstinence-only-until-marriage program providers fail to provide sexuality education that is comprehensive, objective, and appropriate for all young people and that empowers youth to make informed decisions and practice safe and healthy behavior.

Common Characteristics of Abstinence-Only-Until-Marriage Curricula

Abstinence-only-until-marriage program providers in Colorado use many of the same curricula commonly used nationwide, including *WAIT Training*, the *Choosing the Best* series, *Game Plan*, *STARS*, and *ASPIRE: Live Your Life. Be Free*. These curricula promote marriage, rely on messages of fear and shame, and present biased information about gender, sexual orientation, and pregnancy options in a way that is harmful and exclusive to many youth.

SIECUS [Sexuality Information and Education Council of the United States] reviewed the first edition of the *WAIT Training* curriculum and found it to contain little medical or biological information and almost no information about STIs, including HIV/AIDS. It contained information and statistics about marriage, many of which are outdated and not supported by scientific research. Like *WAIT Training* and *ASPIRE*, the *Choosing the Best* series condemns sex before marriage. The series is one of the most popular abstinence-only-until-marriage programs in the country and comprises a number of curricula for students from sixth grade through high school: *Choosing the Best WAY, Choosing the Best PATH, Choosing the Best LIFE, Choosing the Best JOURNEY,* and *Choosing the Best SOUL MATE.*

SIECUS also reviewed *Game Plan* and found that in addition to promoting marriage it fails to provide important information on sexual health including how students can seek testing and treatment if they suspect they may have an STI. Finally, the format and underlying biases of the curriculum do not allow for cultural, community, and individual values, and discourage critical thinking and discussions of alternate points of view in the classroom. For example, *Game Plan* compares sex to fire, noting, "In a fireplace, fire is beautiful and gives warmth to a home. Outside of the fireplace, it can cause serious harm." It continues, "What about sex? In a marriage relationship, sex can be beautiful. Outside of marriage, it can cause serious harm."

The *STARS* curriculum, used in after-school abstinence-only-until-marriage programs, was designed to be implemented by high school student mentors and an adult coordinator to a middle school student audience. The high school mentors are first trained at a four-day national or regional conference run by Friends First [national abstinence-only-until-marriage program provider], at which they are required to sign a pledge to abstain from all sexual activity, drugs, and alcohol while involved in the program. In general, the peer education model has the potential of being a promising way to engage young people; however, like many of the other curricula used in Colorado, this program relies on fear, shame, and a rigid set of values and opinions that it imposes on all students. Very little effort is made to help young people clarify their own values or make decisions for themselves about relationships, and instead, the authors convey messages like "it seems there are pitfalls at every turn in regards to premarital sex," and "as long as students expose themselves to the risks, they will pay the consequences. The consequences of sexually transmitted infections are far greater than the mess of a raw egg. They potentially risk their future fertility and their life!" . . .

Abstinence Education Tries to Remarket Its Programs

The industry is remarkably adaptable and will continue to remarket and rebrand its merchandise to fit the popular thinking and the available federal funding for teen pregnancy prevention and sex education. It has done it before—by removing blatantly religious messages (like the suggestion that young people take Jesus Christ on their dates for protection) and ridiculous medical misinformation (like the idea that young people who have had sex should wash their genitals with Lysol to prevent STIs) from the curricula—and it's doing it again. Today as the industry scrambles to stay relevant it has begun describing its programs as "holistic" and even comprehensive. But if one looks past their marketing into what these programs are saying to students, the original ideology of abstinence-only-until-marriage programs remain unchanged.

3

Abstinence Is the Best Policy in Preventing Teen Pregnancy

US House of Representatives Committee on Energy and Commerce

The Committee on Energy and Commerce, established in 1795, guides the US House of Representatives in matters relating to commerce, energy policy, and the public's health and marketplace interests.

Every day teens are bombarded with cultural messages promoting behaviors that involve considerable risk, such as smoking, drinking, and sexual activity. The problem—as neuroscientists have shown—is that preteens and teenagers have not fully developed the ability to think ahead and assess any risk factors involved in such behaviors. The high rates of sexually transmitted diseases and teenage pregnancy—750,000 pregnant teens per year—support that scientific research. With regard to sexual activity and the ultimate goal of preventing teen pregnancy, the question becomes, how best to educate teens about the risks involved. The best answer is to teach them how to avoid the risky behavior in the first place. Just as successful public health programs encourage avoidance of smoking, drinking, and drug use, sex education programs should likewise encourage teens and preteens to abstain from sexual activity.

Often overlooked in the debate over teenage pregnancy prevention, and certainly overwhelmed by the practical burdens of what is a serious public health issue, is an Ameri-

"A Better Approach to Teenage Pregnancy Prevention: Sexual Risk Avoidance," The Policy Series, Vol.1, Issue 2, pp. 6–8; 10–14, July 2012, U.S. House of Representative Committee on Energy and Commerce.

can teenager. Although the social policy and economic ramifications of 750,000 pregnant teens per year are substantial, each of these pregnancies is about an actual teen and his or her ability to manage the complicated risks associated with premarital sexual behavior and how to shoulder the real possibility of an unwanted pregnancy. The decisions and factors that influence these issues are components of the larger problem—a point first recognized in AFLA [Adolescent Family Life Act]. And if solutions are to be found, they must focus on the factors that produce sexual activity and pregnancy among teens. In short, the solution is to find the best approach to protecting teens from high risk behavior.

Researchers and experts in adolescent behavior have been studying teenage risk taking for decades. Since risk is a key factor in teenage pregnancy prevention and a key difference between the SRA [Sexual Risk Avoidance] approach and CSE [Comprehensive Sex Education] approach, theory and research can help determine the better approach. SRA takes a risk avoidance approach to teenage sexual behavior and presents abstinence as the best choice. CSE maintains that teen sexual behavior is inevitable and that teens need to learn risk reduction to avoid unwanted pregnancies. To identify the better approach, three questions need to be addressed:

1. What the experts tell us about adolescents and risk taking

2. What protects teens as they learn to negotiate risk?

3. How do successful public health prevention programs deal with teenage risk?

What Experts Say About Adolescents and Risk Taking

Young people experience profound physical, cognitive, and emotional changes during adolescence. The physical changes are the most obvious, but other changes during adolescence are equally significant, especially those that challenge personal identity and emotional independence. Teenage thinking can be egocentric and unrealistic with little appreciation for how things actually work. Teens test limits and take risks—behavior that is normal and useful during adolescence. However, for many, unsupervised and reckless behavior can often become too risky and even dangerous.

Expecting preteens and teens to assess and reduce those risks by drawing on the medical information learned . . . is inconsistent with both behavioral and neuroscientific research.

In general, teens take more risks than younger and older individuals even as they lack the proper controls to manage them. Behaviors, such as smoking, drinking, driving, and sexual activity involve considerable risk, especially for teens who have not mastered two important skills—planning and risk assessment. According to Dr. Laurence Steinberg, Professor of Psychology at Temple University, the ability to regulate impulse, think ahead, plan, and weigh risk and reward develop gradually in a teen and are often not complete until the mid-twenties. High rates of underage drinking, car accidents, unplanned pregnancy and STIs [sexually transmitted infections] among teens support the view that most teens are unable to manage the risks associated with these behavioral choices even when provided with warnings.

Brain imaging provides new insights into how the teenage brain works. Using magnetic resonance imaging (MRI), neuroscientists have identified two networks in the frontal lobe of the brain that impact teenage behavior and choices. The social and emotional network is immediately changed with the onset of puberty and becomes very sensitive. The cognitive network that governs planning, thinking ahead, and self-regulation ma-tures gradually. Under normal conditions, the cognitive network can regulate the social/emotional network. However, when the social/emotional network is highly activated, they do not work together. The emotional network dominates the cognitive network. The result is that emotion, rather than reason, often influences teen decision making.

Adolescent development is not entirely determined by brain maturation. Teens are affected by social concerns: education, sports, work, friends, social networks, and other cultural influences. However, as they negotiate these concerns, often independent of their parents, they are frequently drawn to risk—like sexual behavior. Expecting preteens and teens to assess and reduce those risks by drawing on the medical information learned in a few sessions of CSE is inconsistent with both behavioral and neuroscientific research. . . .

An abstinence choice ensures that teens will avoid risky sexual behavior that they are not prepared to handle.

As developmental psychologists, educators, public health experts, and now neuroscientists have discovered, while teens are maturing physically and emotionally and becoming more independent, they are not yet adults. Teens need guidance to make healthy choices. As those choices get more risky and dangerous, guidance and limits from parents that are reinforced by peers, teachers, and other authority figures are critically important.

Public Health Programs Promote Abstaining from Risk Behaviors

Public health programs designed to encourage teens to avoid risk behaviors, such as underage drinking, illicit drug use, and reckless driving have several common elements:

- They work to achieve a maximum level of safety for the teen and the community.

- They encourage risk avoidance and ban or restrict participation in the risky behavior.

- Because of the inherent complexity of behavioral change, they include social-psychological activities that reinforce the healthy message.

- They encourage guidance, especially parental guidance that helps protect the teen.

- They are theory based and age appropriate.

- They rely on age-appropriate program design and rigorous evaluation to continuously monitor the success of the program—if something does not work, new and more effective strategies are adopted. . . .

These public health campaigns to encourage teens to avoid risk behaviors share common factors that are supported by behavioral theory and rigorous evaluation. The programs are value-based as teens were encouraged to make the healthiest choice by avoiding the risky behavior. At the same time, efforts were made to help build the capacity of the teen using guidance and low risk activities. Activities were age-appropriate and dignified. Programs showed effectiveness in getting the teen to adopt the healthy behavior and in reducing national rates of smoking and reckless driving.

SRA is a better approach to prevent teenage pregnancy than CSE, because it is informed by the best available knowledge base. Even though CSE has some good components, SRA is more grounded in behavioral theory and research, and it incorporates the strategies that have been successful in other youth risk programs. With a clear message that abstinence is the best and safest choice for teens, SRA promotes optimal health. An abstinence choice ensures that teens will avoid risky sexual behavior that they are not prepared to handle. SRAs include protective factors, especially the involvement of parents and other guardians. The values present in SRA programs are consistent with views of parents and the community at large. SRA is age-appropriate and presents sensitive information in a dignified manner. SRA holds the promise of finally impacting the incidence of teenage pregnancy and STIs.

More recent abstinence programs, called Sexual Risk Avoidance (SRA) models, are demonstrating effectiveness.

Past Evaluations on Sex Education Programs Have Been Inadequate

Sex education programs in the 1970s had never demonstrated an impact on teenage behavior. It was a purely educational model that was effective in increasing knowledge, but inadequate in actually changing behavior. In addition, these programs did not impact pregnancy trends and appeared to make the problem worse. From 1970–1990 as the number of these programs increased, so did the rates of teenage pregnancy.

By the 1990s, evaluation of sex education became more rigorous. CSE programs showed some progress in changing teenage attitudes and behavior related to sex. However, these results were often limited and non-sustained. In its forward to the 2007 report, *Emerging Answers: Research Findings on Programs to Reduce Teen Pregnancy and Sexually Transmitted Diseases*, the National Campaign to Prevent Teen and Unplanned Pregnancy stated that "many of these (CSE) programs—even those deemed effective—often have only modest results, many are fragile and poorly-funded, and most of these programs serve only a fraction of all the kids in the area who are at risk."

Evaluation of abstinence programs did not begin in earnest until 1996 when Congress authorized $50 million to evaluate their effectiveness. Once completed, these evaluations found that abstinence programs also did not demonstrate an effect on teenage sexual behavior. However, more recent abstinence programs, called Sexual Risk Avoidance (SRA) models, are demonstrating effectiveness.

For both CSE and SRA, the evaluation models currently in place—typically relying only on an outcome evaluation—lack key elements of an effective evaluation strategy. In order to develop meaningful measurements of these programs' impact on teenage behavior and attitudes, a more comprehensive approach to evaluation is needed.

Although outcome evaluation is very important, this one stage of an evaluation process depends on successful completion of other stages, such as the planning and development of a program. Evaluation is simply a comparison between a strategic plan and the actual impacts of that plan. A program plan must be informed by theory that explicitly and accurately identifies the central question to be examined—the hypothesis. A good evaluation begins during the planning stage, continues through implementation, and concludes with an understanding of why a program succeeded or failed.

The debate about the best approach to teenage pregnancy prevention has centered on one aspect of evaluation, the outcome evaluation, even though program planning and development also need to be evaluated. Planning begins with the identification of the assumptions, goals, objectives, and methods that are guided by theory and the best available research. For sex education, the theory base is adolescent development and the vehicle for achieving the goals and objectives is a curriculum. To ensure that the curriculum is well-designed, the content should be reviewed by experts in adolescent development, parents, teachers, and even teens by conducting a form of evaluation called field testing.

One of the biggest reasons that programs fail can be traced to the improper delivery of services. A process evaluation is a way to determine if and how the program was delivered. Monitoring determines if the services, such as sex education, are delivered according to the program plan. Or, as often happens when programs are offered at multiple locations by different teachers, a process evaluation can determine if the services were implemented consistently. For sex education programs, teachers are a key to proper implementation. It is important that they receive training on how to implement the curriculum to avoid variation that can impact findings.

With proper planning and program delivery, the findings from an outcome evaluation, if correctly designed, will be more reliable. They can be used to understand the effect of the program. In addition, they provide the confidence needed to determine if a program can be improved or replicated.

Avoiding Sexual Risk Is the Best Approach

Central to the evaluation process are the explicit assumptions that are used to identify the hypothesis being tested. If the assumptions are not drawn from the best available theoretical and empirical information, it will be difficult to control the quality of the program and evaluate its effectiveness. And, even if some objectives are met, without explicit assumptions, there is no understanding of why the program worked or did not work.

A better approach is needed that incorporates the capability of teens to manage risk in the same way as programs designed to prevent teenage smoking, underage drinking, and reckless driving.

CSE programs have shown some modest success over the last 20 years, yet they never live up to the hope of consistently impacting rates of teenage pregnancy. Why? Because they are guided by the wrong assumptions. For example, even though experts believe that teens lack certain executive functions, CSE assumes that teens armed with "accurate" medical information and interpersonal skills are able to assess the risk involved with sexual activity and disease prevention. In addition, CSE assumes that teens cannot or will not practice abstinence which is not consistent with the evidence that most teens are choosing abstinence. There is a disconnect between theory and assumption or cause and effect in CSE programs that leads to choosing ineffective strategies. As a result, CSE programs, even with those that have shown a modest effect, do little to inform how and why the change occurred.

Rigorous outcome evaluation is the "gold standard" for determining cause, but it works best when it is aligned with other evaluation steps. Planning and evaluation are needed to adequately inform program development. The planning process ensures that the goals, objectives, and methods for the program are grounded in theory and the best available research. Evaluation is used to determine the effectiveness of the program. In the case of sex education programs, outcome evaluation alone, even if it is rigorous, cannot produce the findings needed to inform policy making. Good evaluation begins with good planning and faithful implementation of a well-designed program.

America's teens need guidance to protect them from the consequences of risky sexual behavior. Unfortunately, the current course of national policy on teenage pregnancy prevention is undermining the desired health outcome. Careful examination of research confirms that a value-neutral and risk reduction approach to sexual behavior is not consistent with teenage behavioral theory and not effective in impacting America's high rates of teenage pregnancy and STIs.

A better approach is needed that incorporates the capability of teens to manage risk in the same way as programs designed to prevent teenage smoking, underage drinking, and reckless driving. Teens are confused by messages that are non-directive about risk taking and optimal health. Instead, they need programs that encourage healthy choices and healthy development.

Sex education policy must reinforce the importance of healthy decisions. The goal is ultimately to make a positive change in cultural norms, similar to that reached by other successful public health campaigns. Teens need guidance from those who believe that they are capable of rising to the high expectations of risk avoidance and that even if they have made risky decisions in the past, they can make healthier ones in the future.

SRA education is a better approach, because it is built on sound theory and empirical evidence. Parents, teens, and others on both sides of the political aisle support it. Thus, SRA education must be the first line of defense in helping improve the health of teens.

4

Abstinence-Only Programs Are Ineffective in Preventing Teen Pregnancy

Kathrin F. Stanger-Hall and David W. Hall

Kathrin F. Stanger-Hall is an assistant professor in the plant bi-ology department at the University of Georgia, and David W. Hall is an associate professor in the genetics department at the University of Georgia.

The United States continues to have a high rate of teenage preg-nancy, substantially higher than that seen in other developed countries. The main cause appears to be a lack of comprehensive sex education for students. Studies show that abstinence-only education rarely has a positive effect on teen sexual activity and, in fact, actually increases the teen pregnancy rate. On the other hand, comprehensive sex education that includes the discussion of abstinence is shown to be most effective in reducing teen preg-nancy.

The appropriate type of sex education that should be taught in U.S. public schools continues to be a major topic of debate, which is motivated by the high teen pregnancy and birth rates in the U.S., compared to other developed coun-tries. Much of this debate has centered on whether abstinence-only versus comprehensive sex education should be taught in public schools. Some argue that sex education that covers safe

Kathrin F. Stanger-Hall and David W. Hall, "Abstinence-Only Education and Teen Preg-nancy Rates: Why We Need Comprehensive Sex Education in the U.S.," PLOS ONE, Vol. 6, pp. 1–2; 6–10, October 14, 2011. Reproduced by permission.

sexual practices, such as condom use, sends a mixed message to students and promotes sexual activity. This view has been supported by the US government, which promotes abstinence-only initiatives through the Adolescent Family Life Act (AFLA), Community-Based Abstinence Education (CBAE) and Title V, Section 510 of the Personal Responsibility and Work Opportunity Reconciliation Act of 1996 (welfare reform), among others. Funding for abstinence-only programs in 2006 and 2007 was $176 million annually (before matching state funds). The central message of these programs is to delay sexual activity until marriage, and under the federal funding regulations most of these programs cannot include information about contraception or safer-sex practices.

The more strongly abstinence is emphasized in state laws and policies, the higher the average teenage pregnancy and birth rate.

States Decide the Type of School Sex Education

The federal funding for abstinence-only education expired on June 30, 2009, and no funds were allocated for the FY [fiscal year] 2010 budget. Instead, a "Labor-Health and Human Services, Education and Other Agencies" appropriations bill including a total of $114 million for a new evidence-based Teen Pregnancy Prevention Initiative for FY 2010 was signed into law in December 2009. This constitutes the first large-scale federal investment dedicated to preventing teen pregnancy through research- and evidence-based efforts. However, despite accumulating evidence that abstinence-only programs are ineffective, abstinence-only funding (including Title V funding) was restored on September 29, 2009 for 2010 and beyond by including $250 million of mandatory abstinence-only funding over 5 years as part of an amendment to the

Senate Finance Committee's health-reform legislation (HR 3590, Amendment #2786, section 2954). This was authorized by the legislature on March 23, 2010.

With two types of federal funding programs available, legislators of individual states now have the opportunity to decide which type of sex education (and which funding option) to choose for their state, while pursuing the ultimate goal of reducing teen pregnancy rates. This large-scale analysis aims to provide scientific evidence for this decision by evaluating the most recent data on the effectiveness of different sex education programs with regard to preventing teen pregnancy for the U.S. as a whole. We used the most recent teenage pregnancy, abortion and birth data from all U.S. states along with information on each state's prescribed sex education approach to ask "what is the quantitative evidence that abstinence-only education is effective in reducing U.S. teen pregnancy rates?" If abstinence education results in teenagers being abstinent, teenage pregnancy and birth rates should be lower in those states that emphasize abstinence more. Other factors may also influence teenage pregnancy and birth rates, including socioeconomic status, education, cultural influences, and access to contraception through Medicaid waivers and such effects must be parsed out statistically to examine the relationship between sex education and teen pregnancy and birth rates. It was the goal of this study to evaluate the current sex-education approach in the U.S., and to identify the most effective educational approach to reduce the high U.S. teen pregnancy rates. Based on a national analysis of all available state data, our results clearly show that abstinence-only education does not reduce and likely increases teen pregnancy rates. Comprehensive sex and/or STD [sexually transmitted disease] education that includes abstinence as a desired behavior was correlated with the lowest teen pregnancy rates across states. In alignment with the *Precaution Adoption Process Model* advocated by the National Institutes of Health we suggest that comprehensive sex and HIV/STD education should be taught as part of the biology curriculum in middle and high school science classes, along with a social studies curriculum that addresses risk-aversion behaviors and planning for the future. . . .

Studies Show Abstinence Education Is Ineffective

After accounting for other factors, the national data show that the incidence of teenage pregnancies and births remain positively correlated with the degree of abstinence education across states: The more strongly abstinence is emphasized in state laws and policies, the higher the average teenage pregnancy and birth rate. States that taught comprehensive sex and/or HIV education and covered abstinence along with contraception and condom use (level 1 sex education; also referred to as "abstinence-plus") tended to have the lowest teen pregnancy rates, while states with abstinence-only sex education laws that stress abstinence until marriage (level 3) were significantly less successful in preventing teen pregnancies. Level 0 [sex education with no mention of abstinence] states present an interesting sample with a wide range of education policies and variable teen pregnancy and birth data. For example, several of the level 0 states (as of 2007) did not mandate sex education, but required HIV education only (e.g. CT, WV). Only three of the level 0 states (IA, NH and NV) mandated both sex education and HIV education, but one of them (NV) did not require that teens learn about condoms and contraception. This state (NV) has the highest teen pregnancy and birth rates in that group. Nevada is also one of only five states (with MD in level 0, CO in level 2, and AZ and UT in level 3) that required parental consent for sex education in public schools instead of an opt-out requirement that is present in all the other states.

The effectiveness of Level 1 (comprehensive) sex education in our nation-wide analysis is supported by [Douglas] Kirby's meta-analysis of individual sex education programs, [Kristen]

Underwood et al.'s analysis of HIV prevention programs, and a recent review by the CDC [Centers for Disease Control and Prevention] taskforce on community preventive services. All these studies suggest that comprehensive sex or HIV education that includes the discussion of abstinence as a recommended behavior, and also discusses contraception and protection methods, works best in reducing teen pregnancy and sexually transmitted diseases.

There is strong public support for comprehensive sex education.

Despite large differences between individual research studies that evaluate specific sex education programs (e.g. sample size, approaches to sex education studied, selection of participants, choice of control groups, types of data, control for cross-talk between students outside of class, etc.), several case studies show that abstinence-only education rarely has a positive effect on teen sexual behavior. . . .

Individual research studies also show that teaching about contraception is generally not associated with increased risk of adolescent sexual activity or sexually transmitted diseases (STDs) as suggested by abstinence-only advocates, and adolescents who received comprehensive sex or HIV education had a lower risk of pregnancy and HIV/STD infection than adolescents who received strict abstinence-only or no sex education at all in the U.S. and in other high-income countries.

High Costs Associated with Abstinence Education

Despite the data showing that abstinence-only education is ineffective, it may be argued that the prescribed form of sex education represents the underlying social values of families and communities in each state, and changing to a more comprehensive sex education curriculum will meet with strong opposition. However, there is strong public support for comprehensive sex education. Approximately 82% of a randomly selected nationally representative sample of U.S. adults aged 18 to 83 years supported comprehensive programs that teach students about both abstinence and other methods of preventing pregnancy and sexually transmitted diseases. In contrast, abstinence-only education programs, received the lowest levels of support (36%) and the highest level of opposition (about 50%).

Abstinence-only programs tend to promote abstinence behavior through emotion, such as romantic notions of marriage, moralizing, fear of STDs, and by spreading scientifically incorrect information.

In addition to the federal and state funds spent on abstinence-only (level 3) education, there are other costs associated with the outcomes of failed sex education and family planning. When deciding state policies on sex education, state legislators should consider these additional costs. For example, based on estimates by the National Campaign To Prevent Teen and Unplanned Pregnancy, teen child bearing (compared to first birth at 20 years or older) in the U.S. cost taxpayers (in direct and indirect costs) more than $9.1 billion in 2004.

Our data show that education (percent of high school graduates taking the SAT [standardized test for college admission]) was not correlated with teen pregnancy rates, but it was positively correlated with teen abortion rates and negatively correlated with teen birth rates. These data can be interpreted in two ways: (1) Pregnant teens who give birth are less likely to finish high school and go on to college (i.e. pregnancy affects education). This is supported by a recent report that showed that teen mothers are more likely to drop out of school: 51% of teen mothers earned their high school diploma by age 22, compared to 89% of women who had not given birth as teens. (2) Teens who are motivated to go to college are not necessarily less likely to get pregnant, but more likely to abort their pregnancies (i.e. educational goal affects the decision of whether to carry a pregnancy to term).

Abstinence Education Cultivates Ignorance

As pointed out by the Society for Adolescent Medicine, the abstinence-only approach (as stressed by level 3 state laws and policies and funded by the federal abstinence-only programs) is characterized by the withholding of information and is ethically flawed. Abstinence-only programs tend to promote abstinence behavior through emotion, such as romantic notions of marriage, moralizing, fear of STDs, and by spreading scientifically incorrect information. For example a Congressional committee report found evidence of major errors and distortions of public health information in common abstinence-only curricula. As a result, these programs may actually be promoting irresponsible, high-risk teenage behavior by keeping teens uneducated with regard to reproductive knowledge and sound decision-making instead of giving them the tools to make educated decisions regarding their reproductive health. The effect of presenting inadequate or incorrect information to teenagers regarding sex and pregnancy and STD protection is long-lasting as uneducated teens grow into uneducated adults: almost half of all pregnancies in the U.S. were unplanned in 2001. Of these three million unplanned pregnancies, $\sim$1.4 million resulted in live births, $\sim$1.3 million ended in abortion, and over 400,000 ended in a miscarriage at a financial cost (direct medical costs only) of $\sim$\$5 billion in 2002.

The U.S. teen pregnancy rate is substantially higher than seen in other developed countries despite similar cultural and socioeconomic patterns in teen pregnancy rates. The difference is not due to the onset of sexual activity. Instead, the main factor seems to be sex education, especially with regard to contraception and prevention of STDs. Sex education in Europe is based on the WHO [World Health Organization] definition of sexuality as a lifelong process, aiming to create self-determined and responsible attitudes and behavior with regard to sexuality, contraception, relationships and life strategies and planning. In general, there is greater and easier access to sexual health information and services for all people (including teens) in Europe, which is facilitated by a societal openness and comfort in dealing with sexuality, by pragmatic governmental policies and less influence by special interest groups. . . .

Our analysis adds to the overwhelming evidence indicating that abstinence-only education does not reduce teen pregnancy rates. Advocates for continued abstinence-only education need to ask themselves: If teens don't learn about human reproduction, including safe sexual health practices to prevent unintended pregnancies and STDs, and how to plan their reproductive adult life in school, then when should they learn it, and from whom?

5

Abstinence Sex Education Programs Should Receive Federal Funding

National Abstinence Education Association

The National Abstinence Education Association (NAEA) offers services for abstinence education organizations, educators, and providers, including advocacy and research on behalf of abstinence education.

So-called comprehensive sex education programs receive a much higher amount of federal funding than do abstinence-centered programs, yet research is showing that abstinence is the message that works. The focus of abstinence-centered education is to provide teens with accurate information about sexual activity and the resulting emotional, social, and economic consequences, as well as to empower them with the skills necessary to choose abstinence as their best health-care decision. Furthermore, a study showed that 70 percent of parents and more than 60 percent of teens believe sex should be reserved for marriage; the federal government should take notice and continue funding abstinence education.

Despite what you may read in the newspapers, there is a growing body of research that confirms that SRA abstinence education decreases sexual initiation, increases abstinent behavior among sexually experienced teens, and/or decreases the number of partners among sexually experienced teens.

And if individuals do initiate sex after being in an SRA abstinence program, they are no less likely to use condoms than anyone else. The promising research to show what most people intuitively know—abstinence works!

Isn't "Abstinence Only" Really a "Just Say No" Message?

No—on both counts. SRA abstinence education, as funded by Congress, has nothing to do with "only" and the message is decidedly more inclusive than "just say no." The term, "abstinence only" is used by opponents to create the false perception that abstinence-centered education is a narrow and unrealistic approach. SRA abstinence education is overwhelmingly more comprehensive and holistic than other approaches and focuses on the real-life struggles that teens face as they navigate through the difficult adolescent years.

SRA abstinence education teaches that "having sex" can potentially affect not only the physical apect of a teen's life but also, as research shows, can have emotional, psychological, social, economic, and educational consequences. That's why topics frequently discussed in an SRA abstinence education class include how to identify a healthy relationship, how to avoid or get out of a dangerous, unhealthy, or abusive relationship, developing skills to make good decisions, setting goals for the future and taking realistic steps to reach them, understanding and avoiding STDs [sexually transmitted diseases], information about contraceptives and their effectiveness against pregnancy and STDs, practical ways to avoid inappropriate sexual advances, and why abstinence until marriage is optimal. So, within an SRA abstinence education program, ALL teens receive all the information they need in order to make healthy choices. SRA curricula is holistic and empowering while presenting all topics within the context of abstinence as the best choice. There's nothing "only" about the abstinence approach!

But I Thought That Students in SRA Abstinence Classes Couldn't Receive Information About Condoms and Contraception

Not true! SRA abstinence classes can explain the various contraceptive choices and how they can reduce the risk of acquiring STDs or getting pregnant. This discussion, however, always stresses the best health choice of abstinence as the only way to prevent all risk. Many so-called comprehensive sex ed curricula mislead students by providing only clinical "perfect use" protection rates for condoms, giving students a false sense of security. By contrast, abstinence programs give students the real-life protection rates that a condom offers. A recent national poll of parents demonstrated that 90% want their children to know about the risks associated with casual sex and the limitations of contraception. They want their children to learn accurate information about condoms and contraception in the manner provided in an SRA abstinence education class. It is also important to note that students who have been a part of an abstinence class are no less likely to use a condom if they become sexually active.

Then How Does Sexual Risk Avoidance (SRA) Education Differ from Sexual Risk Reduction (SRR) "Comprehensive Sex Education"?

There are vast differences between SRA abstinence education and SRR comprehensive sex education. The major distinction is how each approach regards teens. SRA education believes teens can and increasingly do, avoid sex. Discussions empower teens to make the healthiest sexual decision which is to abstain, regardless of their previous sexual experience. By contrast, SRR assumes that teens can't or won't avoid sexual experimentation; so the majority of their time is spent talking about sex—using condoms and other forms of contraception with a view to simply reduce, rather than eliminate, sexual risk for teens.

SRA abstinence curricula discuss many topics that teens confront in the increasingly sexualized culture but always within the context of why abstaining is the best choice. The same is not true for most SRR texts. The most wildly used and recommended SRR curricula may include the word or concept of "abstinence" in their texts, but the concept rarely empowers teens to see its value. In fact, an HHS review of SRR curricula show that, on average, about 5% of their time is devoted to the abstinence message, and rather than clear guidance, the definition of abstinence is often subjectively defined by the student. One popular SRR text promoted by comprehensive sex ed providers, asks students to brainstorm "what sexual behaviors a person could engage in and still be 'abstinent.'" Suggested activities as "cuddling with no clothes on," "masturbating with a partner," "rubbing bodies together," and "touching a partner's genitals" are given as possible abstinent behaviors. Students are sent non-directive and confusing definitions for abstinence that are filled with risk and predictably, the discussion quickly moves to "the endless possibilities of outercourse" and "making the transition from sexual abstinence." By contrast, SRA abstinence education provides a clear risk avoidance definition of abstinence. Alarmingly, SRR curricula present abstinence and condom use as equally "safe" options, promoting dangerous and medically inaccurate information to teens.

The difference is clear. The focus of SRA education is to empower teens to avoid risk by making good health decisions, regardless of their sexual history, contrasted with so-called comprehensive sex education that sets the bar much lower, assuming teens will engage in high risk sexual behavior and focusing merely on reducing the risk of that behavior.

What Is the Priority in Federal Funding for Sex Education?

Funding to promote contraceptives and "safe sex" Sexual Risk Reduction (SRR) education among teens currently receives about 16 times the funding as SRA abstinence education. In addition, SRR has received dramatically more funding than SRA education—even during the Bush years—when funding for SRA was at its highest level in recent years. Despite this funding disparity, SRA abstinence education fits squarely within the public health model for primary prevention and risk avoidance. And with a growing body of research showing its effectiveness, continued funding is not only warranted but also highly advisable to impact and improve teen health in America.

Is It True That Most Schools Teach Sexual Risk Avoidance (SRA) Abstinence Education?

The majority of schools still focus on reducing the risk of sex through contraceptive-based Sexual Risk Reduction (SRR) instruction, rather than the risk avoidance, skill-building message of abstinence. In 1995, only 8% of schools taught abstinence education but 84% taught contraceptive-based instruction. In 2002, 22% taught SRA abstinence education, and 68% taught contraceptive-based SRR instruction. Information only up to the year 2002 is available, but this data indicates that fewer than 1 in 4 students across America are receiving SRA abstinence programs. At least in part because of unequal federal funding between both initiatives, more than two-thirds of all teens receive so-called SRR education, a message that assumes that teens will have sex. The recent increase in federal funding for "comprehensive" sex education, together with the decrease in funding for SRA abstinence education, has likely make the educational disparity even more pronounced and detrimental to the overall sexual health of America's youth.

Does the Abstinence Message Have Any Relevance for Teens That Are Sexually Active?

Absolutely! Sexually experienced teens receive the skills and positive empowerment to make healthier choices in the future as a result of SRA abstinence education. A recently published study shows that the abstinence message is especially relevant for sexually experienced teens. Those enrolled in an SRA program were much more likely to choose to abstain than their sexually experienced peers who did not receive abstinence education. Among teens that have had sex, 55% of boys and 72% of girls wish they had waited. The SRA abstinence message charts the only practical approach away from high-risk behavior and toward a decision that removes future risk for that teen.

Why Does SRA Education Oppose Medical Accuracy?

NAEA [National Abstinence Education Association] strongly believes that all youth-serving organizations should provide accurate information to teens on every topic. Organizations receiving federal funds for pregnancy prevention, HIV/AIDS prevention, and all other programs, including SRA abstinence education, should be held to the same standards of accountability and SRA abstinence organizations share this commitment to medical accuracy.

While ideologically motivated individuals and organizations have tried to assert that inaccurate statements characterize SRA abstinence education, this is simply not true. For example, the 2004 report, *The Content of Federally Funded Abstinence-Only Education Programs*, commissioned by Rep. Henry Waxman and compiled, primarily, by special interest groups who are historic opponents to abstinence, relied upon misrepresentation, distortion, and error rather than an honest appraisal of abstinence education curricula.

Most reports on "medical accuracy" fail to note that CSE curricula regularly exaggerate the effectiveness of condoms, underestimate the risk of certain sexual activities, and infer that sex can be made safe and without consequences as long as a condom is used. One widely used text even warns facilitators not to mention any limitations on condom effectiveness to students.

SRA abstinence education is medically accurate, theoretically sound and consistent with a public health model typically used to address youth risk behaviors.

Why Should the Government Fund SRA Abstinence Education? Isn't That a Separation of Church and State Violation?

The curricular content of SRA abstinence education programs funded by the federal government is consistent with the public health prevention model for risk avoidance. In terms of general public health policy, the best health outcomes are made possible by the best positive health behavior messaging. SRA abstinence education follows this health model, while all other approaches offer a message that still leave youth at risk for some of the consequences of sexual activity. SRA abstinence education provides all the information necessary for teens to make the best choice for their sexual health. The fact that the world's major religions support abstinence until marriage does not disqualify abstinence as an important public health goal.

With Most People Having Sex Before Marriage, Isn't the "Abstinence Until Marriage" Message Unrealistic?

The fact that many individuals have sex before marriage and more than 40% of all births are outside of marriage does not diminish the benefits of waiting to have children until marriage, nor does it mean we should abandon the goal of changing the cultural norm for this behavior. In fact, historically, if a cultural behavior or norm is in conflict with the desired outcome, efforts are redoubled, not abandoned. For example, a generation ago, smoking was a desired, normative behavior, but today smoking is almost universally viewed as undesirable and unhealthy proof that cultural and social norms do change. Similarly, although growing numbers of Americans are over-weight, efforts to encourage exercise and healthy eating habits have increasingly become public health priority messages. We do not capitulate our highest public health standards based on the unhealthy choices of a majority, but on standards that promote optimal health outcomes in the population.

Overwhelming social science data reveals that children who are born within a committed married relationship fare better economically, socially, physically, and psychologically. In terms of child outcomes, the facts are clear—waiting until af-ter marriage to have children is indisputably in the child's best interest. Further, most teens are not sexually active and more and more teens are choosing to be abstinent, proving that the message of abstinence increasingly resonates with youth. Am-plified efforts to link the personal benefits of abstinence with the positive effects for children born from a marital union are warranted and necessary if positive changes in cultural norms are to be realized.

I've Heard That Most Parents Want Their Children to Receive SRR "Comprehensive Sex Education" Rather than SRA "Abstinence Education". Isn't SRA Abstinence Education Out of Touch with What Parents Want Their Children to Be Taught?

A study posted to the U.S. Dept of Health and Human ser-vices website in August 2010 showed that 70% of parents and more than 60% of teens believe that sex should be reserved for marriage. Sexual Risk Avoidance education is the only sex education approach that provides youth the skills to reach this goal. Additionally, when parents understand the differences between SRR and SRA curricula, they prefer abstinence education to so-called comprehensive sex education by a 2:1 margin.

Parents across all ideological, political, and demographic boundaries want what is best for their children and in terms of sexual health; the favored approach is SRA abstinence-centered education.

6

Comprehensive Sex Education Programs Should Receive Federal Funding

Jendayi Phillip

Jendayi Phillip, a student at Howard University pursuing a degree in psychology with a focus on reproductive health policy, has previously been an intern with the Reproductive Health Technologies Project and a public policy intern at the Advocates for Youth organization.

More than 60 percent of school-aged children in the United States are having sex, and because it is their right to lead healthy lives, they need to receive medically accurate comprehensive sexual health education. Federal funding to institutions—such as departments of education, nonprofit organizations, local and tribal organizations, and departments of health—that teach comprehensive sex education is vital to ensure young people receive the skills and information necessary to make responsible and healthy decisions. The Real Education for Healthy Youth Act would ensure that outcome.

The Real Education for Healthy Youth Act (S. 1782/H.R. 3324), introduced by Senator Frank Lautenberg (D-NJ) and Representative Barbara Lee (D-CA), would ensure that federal funding is allocated to comprehensive sexual health education programs that provide young people with the skills and information they need to make informed, responsible, and healthy decisions. This legislation sets forth a vision for comprehensive sexual health education programs in the United States.

What Would the Real Education for Healthy Youth Act Do?

The Real Education for Healthy Youth Act outlines criteria for content in federally funded sex education programs. The bill outlines a holistic approach to sexual health and provides funding for comprehensive sexual health education programs which:

- Recognize young people's right to sexual health information;

- Define comprehensive sexual health education programs as those which include information on:

  - anatomy and physiology

  - growth and development

  - healthy relationships

  - prevention of unintended pregnancy and sexually transmitted infections (STIs), including HIV, through abstinence and contraception

  - gender, gender identity, and sexual orientation

  - protection from dating violence, sexual assault, bullying, and harassment;

- Are evidence-based, or include characteristics of effective programs that have proven effective in changing the sexual behavior of young people;

- Provide medically accurate and age-appropriate information; and

- Are inclusive of lesbian, gay, bisexual, and transgender (LGBT) youth.

Who Is Provided Funding Under the Real Education for Healthy Youth Act?

Federal funding would be provided to institutions teaching comprehensive sexual health education to adolescents and college students, including departments of education; non-profit organizations; state, local and tribal organizations; departments of health; and institutions of higher education. Priority in funding is given to communities with high rates of health disparities in unintended pregnancy, STIs, and dating violence and sexual assault, as well as institutions of higher education that serve a large number of students of color and Pell grant [federal grants to students of low income families] recipients. In addition to grants for educating young people, funding is directed to pre-service and in-service teacher training for K-12 sex educators to increase effective teaching of comprehensive sexual health education.

Of those [teens] who gave birth, 50 percent were not using birth control and 31 percent of these believed they could not get pregnant.

Why Is the Real Education for Healthy Youth Act Necessary?

Sixty-three percent of young people will have sex before they graduate high school and 95 percent will have sex before they are married. For young people to make healthy decisions about sex, we need to provide them the skills and information they need.

Young people are disproportionately impacted by STIs, including HIV, and unintended pregnancy.

- Approximately 40 percent of sexually active students reported not using condoms at last intercourse.

- It is estimated that close to 750,000 teens become pregnant each year.

- The United States has the highest teen pregnancy rate (72 pregnancies per 1000 young women ages 15–19) of developed nations, with a teen pregnancy rate over four times that of the Netherlands (14), over three times that of Germany (19), and almost three times that of France (26).

- Approximately 400,000 teens every year give birth in the U.S. Of those who gave birth, 50 percent were not using birth control and 31 percent of these believed they could not get pregnant.

- The CDC [Centers for Disease Control and Prevention] reports that young people ages 15–24 account for almost half of the 19 million new STIs every year.

- Young people ages 13–29 account for 39 percent of new HIV infections.

- Youth of color are disproportionately affected by the HIV/AIDS epidemic. Young African Americans accounted for 65 percent of HIV diagnoses among those 13–24. African American/Black young men who have sex with men (YMSM) accounted for nearly 63 percent of all YMSM ages 13–24 with HIV infection in 2009, followed by white YMSM (18 percent) and Hispanic/Latino YMSM (16 percent).

Comprehensive sexual health education helps reduce the rates of STIs and unintended pregnancy among young people by providing complete and accurate information to help young people make responsible, informed decisions about sex and healthy relationships. Research has shown effective sex education programs have positive outcomes among young people such as delaying the initiation of sex, decreasing the number of sexual partners, and increasing the use of contraception and condoms. Yet, the government still allocates millions of dollars to abstinence-only-until-marriage programs. In fact, research has shown that young people in abstinence-only-until-marriage programs that promote "virginity pledges" still engage in sexual activity before marriage and are less likely to protect themselves when they do have sex.

Public opinion polls have consistently demonstrated that the majority of Americans support the teaching of comprehensive sex education to our nation's young people.

Surveys on research of youth around our nation have also reported high rates of bullying, harassment and dating violence.

- Eight out of ten LGBT students reported being harassed in the last year, three-fifths reported feeling unsafe, and one-third skipped at least one day of school in the past month because of concerns about their safety.

- Surveys show that 8 percent of high school students have been forced to have intercourse and 9 percent have experienced dating violence.

Comprehensive sex education can help combat the rise in dating violence and bullying among youth. Studies have led researchers to recommend that information on healthy relationships be integrated into sex education programs. One study reported that students were 60 percent less likely to perpetrate forms of dating violence against a partner after being taught a safe dating curriculum. Research has also demonstrated that students positively benefit from an LGBT inclusive curriculum. Furthermore, students who attend LGBT inclusive schools are less likely to feel unsafe at school because of their sexual orientation (42 percent vs. 64 percent) or gender expression (28 percent vs. 41 percent) and about half as likely to miss school because of feeling unsafe or uncomfortable (17 percent vs. 31 percent).

What Is the Public Opinion on Comprehensive Sexual Health Education?

Public opinion polls have consistently demonstrated that the majority of Americans support the teaching of comprehensive sex education to our nation's young people. Over 80 percent of Americans favor courses that teach contraception and disease prevention in addition to abstinence, and close to 70 percent oppose federal funding for programs that do not teach about condoms and contraception. Furthermore, studies show that 90 percent of the engaged public supports age-appropriate and medically accurate sex education for all students beginning in early grades and up into high schools and close to 70 percent oppose federal funding for programs that do not teach about condoms and contraception.

Support exists across party lines for comprehensive sex education. According to a recent poll, 75 percent of Republicans, 79 percent of Independents, and 85 percent of Democrats support it. Of those who identify with the Tea Party, 54 percent favor the teaching of comprehensive sex education. There is also strong support across religious groups with 78 percent of Catholics, 74 percent of black Protestants, and 62 percent of white evangelicals in favor of teaching comprehensive sex education in public schools.

Young people have the right to lead healthy lives. Providing them with honest, age appropriate comprehensive sexual health education is an integral part of helping them take personal responsibility for their health and well-being.

7

Most US Parents Favor Abstinence Sex Education Programs

National Abstinence Education Foundation

The National Abstinence Education Foundation provides educational, media, and research efforts to ensure young people receive Sexual Risk Avoidance (SRA) Abstinence Education on a nationwide basis.

In order to clarify what type of sex education most parents want for their children, a survey was conducted so that US policy makers could respond to the opinions of this important constituency. The results clearly reveal widespread support by parents for the messages and goals taught in abstinence education programs. Some of these lessons include the limitations of condoms; the potential long-term emotional consequences that can accompany teen sex; the only safe way to avoid sexually transmitted diseases is through abstinence; and that abstinence until marriage offers the best outcomes for men, women, and children. Furthermore, the survey results endorse abstinence education as the preferred choice among parents across all demographics that were studied.

*P*arents Speak Out is a national survey of American parents that was commissioned and released by the National Abstinence Education Foundation (NAEF). The survey asked parents a series of questions that revealed their general views on sex education, with specific questions designed to ascertain support or lack of support for topics commonly covered in the Sexual Risk Avoidance (SRA) Abstinence Education approach. In addition, it asked parents to give their opinions regarding recent sex education policy decisions that have been recommended and implemented by the [Barack] Obama Administration, as well as policy initiatives introduced by members of Congress.

Parents also believe it is important for teens to know that most of their peers are not having sex.

Attempting to Clarify the Views of Parents

The purpose of *Parents Speak Out* is to clarify the views of parents regarding the sex education of their children so that policy-makers at the local, state, and national levels can be responsive to the opinions of this very important constituency. NAEF wanted to know whether support for the SRA Abstinence Approach generally divided along party lines, or whether parents spoke in unison for the type of sex education information they want for their children.

The unprecedented elimination of abstinence education programs by the Obama administration marked a stunning departure from bipartisan approval of abstinence education funding in previous Democratic and Republican administrations. The anti-abstinence actions by the Obama administration also sharpened the brewing political divide in Washington, DC, over sex education. However, NAEF has long held that support for SRA Abstinence Education programs crosses party lines—and that the anti-abstinence policies of the Obama administration are out of step, not only with best health outcomes for America's youth, but also with what their political base wants for their own children.

Since *both* Sexual Risk Reduction (SRR) "Comprehensive" Sex Education and SRA Abstinence Education regularly provide information on contraception to teens (particularly condom information), NAEF wanted to know which approach for giving this information was most in line with how parents wanted the information to be communicated. Specifically, do they favor the typical SRA Abstinence Education approach, informing teens that, while condoms reduce their risk of acquiring sexually transmitted diseases (STD) and pregnancy, condoms also possess limitations, and that even sex with condoms carries risk? Or do parents favor the SRR "Comprehensive" Sex Education approach, which sometimes cautions teachers against sharing any of condoms' limitations, for fear that teens will then be less likely to use them if they do become sexually active? . . .

NAEF was not surprised that this most recent survey of parents' beliefs about their children's sex education showed widespread support by parents for the tenets of SRA Abstinence Education. Earlier surveys, conducted by both NAEF and the US Department of Health and Human Services, indicated strong support for the abstinence until marriage message by parents. However, we were surprised at how widespread the support was among all the major demographics that were studied in this survey. Specifically, the answers to the questions we posed at the outset of the survey were answered in an astonishing and overwhelming pro-SRA Abstinence Education manner. . . . The key findings are specifically described below.

Support for the SRA Abstinence Approach Transcends Party Lines

Parents from both parties favor SRA Abstinence Education for their teens. Republicans and Democrats support the way that Abstinence Education addresses key topics. They want sex education to place a priority on encouraging teens to avoid sex in order to avoid all sexual risk. Parents also believe it is important for teens to know that most of their peers are *not having sex*. Parents believe that sexually experienced students deserve to know that they can still benefit by choosing abstinence from this point forward in their relationships. Parents favor sex education classes that teach students about the limitations of condoms, as well as the causes, symptoms, and best way to avoid the transmission of STDs, which of course, is abstinence.

Support for abstinence education crossed all racial lines.

Democrats and Republicans alike want sex education classes to address holistic topics typically included in SRA Abstinence Education classes. Therefore, as the survey findings indicate, they believe it is important for discussions to go beyond dialogs regarding the physical consequences of teen sex. They want their children to know about the potential emotional consequences that can accompany teen sex, the practical skills associated with healthy decision-making, and requisite skills to develop healthy relationships. Parents also believe it is important for students to know that if they engage in risk behaviors, such as smoking or teen sex, students may have more difficulty reaching their goals.

Parents support the manner in which SRA Abstinence Education discusses condom information with teens rather than the manner in which many SRR "Comprehensive" Sex Education programs discuss condoms. Parents overwhelmingly want their chidren to know about the limitations of condom effectiveness—information that is often not shared in a typcial SRR "Comprehensive" Sex Education program. In fact, parents feel so strongly about this key component of sex education, that they scored this response higher than any other question of the survey. It is also of interest to note that both Democrats and Republicans score this question very similarly.

Parents Want Children to Delay Sex Until Marriage

Most parents want their children to wait until marriage before they engage in sex. Parents overwhelmingly indicated a desire that their children wait until they marry before engaging in sex. Despite the fact that abstinence education critics insist that "abstinence until marriage" is outdated, parents do not agree. Perhaps parents know that social science research clearly supports this context for sex as offering the best outcomes for women, men, and children born of their sexual unions. The survey results suggest that while all demographic groups support the concept of "abstinence until marriage" by a large margin, African American parents appear to overwhelmingly desire that their children wait for marriage to initiate sex. . . .

Support for abstinence education crossed all racial lines, but support among African American parents was especially striking. Unfortunately, teen pregnancy rates among African American girls are high and the CDC [Centers for Disease Control and Prevention] estimates that one in two African American teen girls has *at least* one STD, compared to one in four teen girls overall. Not surprisingly, concern for teen sexual activity is of special concern among African American parents. One parent expressed support for abstinence education as the most effective pregnancy prevention program as follows: "*I wish the government would help support [abstinence education] so we would have less child-on-child pregnancies, because it's difficult to raise a child at a teen age. It destroys their life and it makes them where they cannot finish school or proceed.*" Parents agreed that abstinence is the best choice for their children and hoped they would wait until married before becoming sexually active. White and Hispanic parents agreed, and one Hispanic parent stated forthrightly: "*Abstinence is very good for our youth.*" The level of support was highest among African American parents.

Current policies that ignore the need to include a clear priority on risk avoidance to all teens, regardless of sexual orientation, should be immediately amended.

When asked about their support for specific abstinence education themes, African American parents, in general, were more supportive than parents overall.

Abstinence Education Benefits Gay Youth

Most parents believe gay youth can benefit from abstinence education. Parents believe it is important for all teens to receive the information and skills to wait for sex, regardless of their sexual orientation. Unfortunately, few programs that target gay teens center on risk avoidance, a policy that is out of step with the desires of most parents. Democrats typically communicate that they have a unique concern for the health of homosexual youth. Yet this survey indicates that Republican parents were very supportive of protecting *all teens* from the inherent risks associated with teen sex, without regard to their sexual orientation. This phenomenon is true even more so, in fact, than for their comparative Democratic counterparts. . . .

The broad support for providing all teens, regardless of sexual orientation with skills to help them avoid sexual risk should speak to HIV/AIDS activists who spurn abstinence education under the mistaken pretense that the messages have no relevance to this important subgroup. Parents have come alongside conventional public health priorities that encourage the best health outcomes for all targeted populations. Current policies that ignore the need to include a clear priority on risk avoidance to all teens, regardless of sexual orientation, should be immediately amended. Such amendments can be implemented with confidence knowing that public health protocols should demand such a change and that parents also support these messages for their children.

Social Science Research Supports Abstinence Education

Parents widely support their teens waiting until marriage before engaging in sex. Perhaps parents see, as social science research supports, that the goals for SRA Abstinence Education provide a true opportunity to improve the advantage their children will have for future success. Abstinence until marriage is overwhelmingly supported by social science research. Policymakers should refuse to be intimidated by special interest groups who are willing and all too eager to ignore the benefits of bearing children in marriage.

The *Parents Speak Out* survey results should provide a wake-up call to policy leaders in Washington, DC, and across the nation. The results clearly reveal that many leaders are out of touch with what parents and *their own constituency and support* base favor regarding sex education. The results of the present study clearly communicate that the political divide over sex education is misguided. Bipartisan support for SRA Abstinence Education should increase, and champions on both sides of the aisle should share these findings with their colleagues. The survey results provide a strong endorsement of SRA Abstinence Education as a preferred choice for sex education. Parents and policymakers alike should be encouraged that this support is in good company with a deep bench of research-informed practices, theories, and implementation strategies that offer the best sexual health outcomes for America's youth.

8

Abstinence Education Programs Incorporate Shame and Guilt

Calah Alexander

Calah Alexander is the author of the blog Barefoot and Pregnant *on Patheos.com, a website dedicated to discussions of religion and spirituality.*

Simply put, abstinence-only education causes harm. Not only does it fail to give youth accurate information about human sexuality, abstinence education perpetuates a chauvinistic culture. Using lessons that compare unmarried girls who have had sex to chewed-up pieces of gum or tainted glasses of water, abstinence-only education instills feelings of worthlessness and shame that can continue even after marriage. To protect young people from continued psychological and emotional damage, sex education courses should focus on the positive aspects of human sexuality and how to properly integrate them into life, both outside and inside of marriage.

L ast week [May 2013], the conservative circles of the internet were abuzz in disapproval over Elizabeth Smart's [who was kidnapped and sexually abused at age fourteen] recent criticism of abstinence-only sexual education. Speaking at a forum on human trafficking at Johns Hopkins University, Elizabeth said that the abstinence-only education she received left her feeling "so dirty" and "so filthy" after being repeatedly raped.

The reactions to this were infuriatingly predictable. Good people, people who have proven to be thoughtful and compassionate, immediately shut down in the face of any criticism of abstinence-only sex ed. Their responses to Elizabeth Smart were irrational, ignorant, and stunningly condescending. From accusing her of "casting blame" to snarkily suggesting that we teach "bestiality (oral, anal, etc . . .) as an alternative to those worthless, dirty, filthy feelings," there was a mob-like mentality on display. People stubbornly defended her religious parents and reminded each other how she had held on through her captivity so she could get back to them, without bothering to explain what that had to do with the point she was making. People insisted that the shame and unworthiness she felt was solely the result of the abuse she suffered, and by making her emotional trauma about abstinence-only education she was doing a disservice to other forms of abuse. People claimed that she was using her platform irresponsibly, and should have thought through the impact her words would have on the abstinence-only sex ed movement.

Abstinence Education from a Personal Viewpoint

What almost no one did was hear what she said. No one was horrified at what she had been taught in her abstinence-only sexual education. No one acknowledged that the direct, logical result of such an education is a sense of shame and unworthiness after having been "used." No one showed even a hint of sympathy for how she had suffered, not only at the hands of her captors, but at the hands of a degrading philosophy of human sexuality. Such a callous indifference to human suffering is appalling. It shows that too many Christians, too many proponents of abstinence-only education, have put their concern for the welfare of a quasi-political movement above their concern for the welfare of a human being, of human dignity itself.

For some time, I have thought that the reason more people aren't speaking out against this "purity culture" is that they are unaware of it. After last week, I'm not so sure. The mainstream message of abstinence-only education got press far and wide with Elizabeth Smart's denunciation of it, yet I saw no shock, horror, or disgust.

Let me be clear about the particular type of abstinence-only education Elizabeth Smart is referring to. I'm not entirely convinced that there is another type, but just in case, this is the abstinence-only message that Elizabeth Smart received as an adolescent: Smart said she grew up in a Mormon family and was taught through abstinence-only education that a person whose virginity was lost before marriage was considered worthless. She spoke to the crowd about a school teacher who urged students against premarital sex and compared women who had sex before their wedding nights to chewing gum.

> I thought, "Oh my gosh, I'm that chewed up piece of gum, nobody re-chews a piece of gum. You throw it away." And that's how easy it is to feel like you no longer have worth, you no longer have value. Why would it even be worth screaming out? Why would it even make a difference if you are rescued? Your life still has no value.

Perhaps there are some people out there who think this mindset is an abberration, who are not responding to this because they genuinely believe this is a rare exception to typical abstinence-only curricula. It isn't.

Abstinence Education Denigrates Sexuality

It is absolutely crucial that Catholics, Christians, and all proponents of abstinence-only education get their heads out of the sand on this. This is not some sort of freaky Mormon glitch in the abstinence-only train. This IS the abstinence-only train.

When I heard it, it was glasses of water. Women (and only women, mind you; the boys got a separate talk about cherishing each woman as if she were the prized treasure of another man) were like glasses of crystal-clear spring water. If you "fooled around" before marriage, it was like someone spit in your glass of water. If you had sex before marriage, it was like someone took a huge drink of your water, swished it around in their mouths, and then spat it back into the glass. The more sex you had, the dirtier your glass of water got. "So think of that before you have premarital sex," we were admonished. "Think of the gift you're going to give your husband on your wedding night. Do you want to give him a pure, untouched glass of delicious water, or a dirty cup of everyone else's backwash?"

Girls are told over and over in abstinence-only education that sex before marriage will make them dirty and worthless.

For one of my friends, it was an Oreo cookie that had been chewed up and spat back out. For another friend, it was a pair of custom-made shoes that had been stretched and warped from being worn by people they weren't made to fit. Cups of spit. Plucked roses. It goes on and on. I've heard a million variations of it, but always the message is the same.

This does not teach anyone chastity or purity. "Abstinence-only" sex ed is a fundamentally flawed concept, beginning with its very name. It teaches children to negate an act, to deny a fundamental part of human nature until such a time as it's permissible to indulge. It doesn't teach children what sex is, what their sexuality means, how to understand it, or how to properly integrate it into a life of chastity both without and within a marriage. It doesn't teach a boy that sex is primarily about the giving of himself, and that he can't fully give himself to his wife unless he learns how to master himself first, how to wait, how to have patience, how to love her instead of using her as a vehicle for pleasure. Actually it teaches boys the exact opposite of that; that a woman is a trophy, a prize, that a good one (one worth keeping forever) will be untouched, but that there are plenty of dirty water-glasses walking around that have been ruined for any decent man anyway, and they might as well be used up since they're not worth saving.

Sex Education Should Emphasize the Positive

And what does abstinence-only sex ed teach girls? It doesn't *teach* girls anything. It *conditions* girls into conforming with a sick, "religious-ized" chauvinism that masquerades as concern for moral purity but is really just plain old abhorrence of sloppy seconds. It says nothing to a girl about her inherent value as a human being, about her precious and vital role as life-giver, about her unique feminine genius that is inextricably linked to her sexuality. Like Pavlov's dog, girls are told over and over in abstinence-only education that sex before marriage will make them dirty and worthless. The conditioning definitely works as intended on us pieces of chewed-up gum; our sexual relationships within marriage are usually fraught with psychological blocks, feelings of worthlessness, and fears of abandonment. It also does a number on girls who have been raped, like Elizabeth Smart. But here's the thing: it totally screws up the "good" girls, too, the ones who wait until their wedding night. You can't tell a girl that having sex is like being a chewed and regurgitated Oreo and then expect her to be totally excited when it comes time for her husband to chew her up and spit her back out. You can't teach a girl that her sexuality is a prize for a man, that the whole purpose of her existence as a sexual being is to be used by someone else at the "right" time and in the "right" way, and then wonder where these silly girls get their "objectification" martyr complexes.

It's time to have a serious conversation about abstinence-only sex ed, and how it is not only failing but damaging our youth. It is screwing up our cultural understanding of human sexuality just as thoroughly as the hedonistic effects of the sexual revolution are. There very well may be some good abstinence-only sex ed courses out there, but they are certainly not the norm. We need to create a new way of teaching children about human sexuality, a way that emphasizes their essential dignity as rational, spiritual, and sexual human beings. We should strive to teach them to grow in virtue, to gain temperance, to master their passions, and to love *for love of the other*, not out of desire for pleasure, power, or possession. We should be teaching human sexuality as a series of positive moral developments that boys and girls must attain before sex can be truly enjoyed. We shouldn't be teaching our kids to white-knuckle it through puberty and then glut themselves as soon as they say "I do."

> *There are two whole generations of young adults who have been psychologically and emotionally damaged by the widespread and complacent acceptance of abstinence-only sex ed.*

Abstinence Education Does Not Educate

The question is not whether or not abstinence-only education is working. I'm not even sure what proponents of it mean by "working." In the incarnation I'm familiar with, it certainly doesn't seem intended to do much beyond shaming kids into not having sex using the crudest, most psychologically destructive means available. Research is pretty clear that it's not even managing to accomplish that. The only thing abstinence-only education is accomplishing is entrenching misogynistic, licentious attitudes toward sex in a whole new generation of kids.

There is no excuse for Christians to close their eyes and pretend that abstinence-only sex ed is even a tolerable thing, much less a good thing. This dehumanizing approach to sexuality is not an acceptable alternative to the Planned Parenthood-driven over-sexualization of our kids. I will not settle for my kids learning anything less than the full theology of the body, and neither should you. You don't need to defend abstinence-only sex ed from attacks by girls like Elizabeth Smart; you need to defend girls like Elizabeth Smart from the psychological effects of abstinence-only sex ed. It is not "education" in any sense of the word. It is shallow, sickening cultural conditioning, and we owe our kids enough to admit it. There are two whole generations of young adults who have been psychologically and emotionally damaged by the widespread and complacent acceptance of abstinence-only sex ed. Let's not make it three.

9

Abstinence Education Programs Do Not Incorporate Shame and Guilt

Valerie Huber and Greg Pfundstein

Valerie Huber is president of the National Abstinence Education Association (NAEA), an advocacy organization on behalf of abstinence education. Greg Pfundstein is a board member of the NAEA and president of the Chiaroscuro Foundation, a nonprofit organization that seeks to reduce the number of abortions in New York State.

Much of the criticism directed at abstinence education programs is based on misinformation and misunderstanding. For example, it has been said that abstinence education uses shame, shows a lack of compassion, and teaches a flawed view of human sexuality in its curriculum. The truth is, however, that abstinence educators communicate the beauty of human sexuality and help teens understand that their value and self-worth are not dependent on having sex. Furthermore, abstinence education does not demean those teens who have already had sex or treat them as "sloppy seconds," but rather affirms their dignity and encourages them to choose abstinence in the future.

Abstinence education has long been attacked from the left with a creative array of misinformation. Perhaps the most common attack against abstinence education is that it "doesn't

Valerie Huber and Greg Pfundstein, "Not Used Up: Progress in Abstinence Education," *Public Discourse*, Witherspoon Institute, June 3, 2013. Copyright © 2013 by Witherspoon Institute. All rights reserved. Reproduced by permission.

work." Another top contender is the claim that abstinence education is a thinly veiled program aimed at indoctrinating unsuspecting American children in a biblical worldview; since government resources are used in government facilities, this constitutes a clear establishment of religion and a violation of the First Amendment, or so the argument goes.

Criticism Aimed at Abstinence Education

For veterans of this corner of the culture war, it has been interesting to read a veritable outburst of criticism of abstinence education from conservative religious people who are claiming that abstinence education is not religious enough.

The recent criticism came in response to comments made by Elizabeth Smart, who was kidnapped from her home at age fourteen and held for nine months, during which time she experienced the horror of sexual slavery. Speaking at a forum on human trafficking at Johns Hopkins University, she recalled being told by a schoolteacher that a person who has had sex is like a piece of chewed gum. Smart said that the idea contributed to her despair while held captive:

> I thought, "Oh, my gosh, I'm that chewed up piece of gum, nobody re-chews a piece of gum, you throw it away." And that's how easy it is to feel like you no longer have worth, you no longer have value.... Why would it even be worth screaming out? Why would it even make a difference if you are rescued? Your life still has no value.

While we don't know Smart's opinion on the subject, her comments were immediately taken up as weapons in the fight over sex education. According to critics, Smart's comments are definitive proof that abstinence education is bad, bad, bad. No surprise there. More interesting, however, was the response from conservative people of faith.

Perhaps the most circulated article in the genre is "Sloppy Seconds Sex Ed" by Calah Alexander blogging at *Patheos*. She argued that the defensive response of many religious conservatives showed a lack of compassion, but also a flawed view of human sexuality. "It shows that too many Christians, too many proponents of abstinence-only education, have put their concern for the welfare of a quasi-political movement above their concern for the welfare of a human being, of human dignity itself," Alexander wrote. . . .

The abstinence education movement began because educators were concerned that teens were not receiving the skills they needed to avoid all the risks associated with sex.

Alexander goes on to allow that maybe there is another perspective on the subject that she is not hearing, though she quickly dismisses the possibility: "Perhaps there are some people out there who think this mindset is an aberration, who are not responding to this because they genuinely believe this is a rare exception to typical abstinence-only curricula."

That's our cue. It is always dangerous to poll a handful of friends and draw conclusions. While no one can vouch for every abstinence program that has been used by well-intentioned presenters over the last two decades, we can confidently say that the sort of demeaning messages received by Smart and others are outside the mainstream of state-of-the-art abstinence-education programs.

Background Information on the Abstinence Education Movement

It might help to consider the history of abstinence education. About thirty years ago, the abstinence education movement began because educators were concerned that teens were not receiving the skills they needed to avoid all the risks associated with sex.

Efforts were made to communicate the wonder and beauty of sex along with the potential risks of pregnancy and disease that often accompany teen sexual activity.

They were similarly concerned that the sexual "double standard" still provided too much of the narrative for the expected behavior of too many teens. This "double standard" deemed sexual experimentation among boys a "rite of passage" and a sign of virility, whereas sexual experimentation among girls was proof of their loose morals. Along with this corrupted characterization of sexuality was an assumption that teen sexual activity was inevitable and that the solution was to provide condoms under the pretense that sex would then be "safe."

From the beginning, abstinence educators believed that sexual delay was the optimal choice for all teens. They believed that teen pregnancy prevention programs were insufficient and did more to normalize sex among teens than to empower them to wait, even as social science research was replete with evidence that encouraging teens to wait for sex until marriage was the best choice.

Therefore efforts were made to communicate the wonder and beauty of sex along with the potential risks of pregnancy and disease that often accompany teen sexual activity. In the age of AIDS and an overall teen STD [sexually transmitted disease] epidemic, it was and remains an important task to share the reality of disease transmission with vulnerable teens in a concrete manner.

In the past thirty years, abstinence programs have come a very long way from their beginnings. So far, in fact, that many practitioners have adopted an entirely new name for the programs they run: Sexual Risk Avoidance Programs. There are now many Sexual Risk Avoidance (SRA) programs in use that are medically accurate and based on sound public health and behavioral models, all supported by solid methodology and pedagogy.

Regardless of what you have done in the past, the optimal choice for your health is to choose to be abstinent in the future.

Positive Outcomes Associated with Abstinence Education

The great improvements that have come with this experience have reaped notable rewards. There are now twenty-three studies either published in peer-reviewed academic journals or reported to the government that show statistically significant effects on various measures of success for sex education programs, such as delayed sexual debut, decreased number of sexual partners, and even increased use of condoms and contraceptives, typical measures that indicate the approach "works."

Strong SRA programs go well beyond the straw-man "just say no" approach. They also aim to inspire young men and women to set positive goals for their futures. Choosing to wait for sex is an important decision in that process, though not the only one. SRA programs help teens understand that their value is not dependent on whether they have sex with their date; they aim to help teens develop aspirations that transcend the pressure to be sexually active at a young age.

Perhaps most relevant to the current controversy is the fact that the SRA approach is the only one that believes in "another chance" for any individual who has made unhealthy decisions in the past. Far from being "used up," teens are given renewed hope for starting over. "Renewed abstinence" is an articulated goal of SRA programs, and there is some evidence that it is easier to get young people to choose renewed abstinence than to get them to use condoms.

A study conducted in Uganda, for example, found that young people were substantially more likely to stop having sex for long periods after their first sexual debut than to use condoms. SRA programs take the commonsense public-health approach: Regardless of what you have done in the past, the optimal choice for your health is to choose to be abstinent in the future.

Of course, SRA programs also help teens know how to differentiate between healthy and unhealthy relationships, how best to avoid STDs, and how to avoid sexual advances. These same programs are quick to refer teens who have been victimized by sexual abuse for legal and counseling help. And it is important to note that many abstinence programs are at work in communities where young people are at much higher risk of the negative outcomes associated with teen sexual activity.

SRA educators should recognize effective teaching methods and have access to the most up-to-date scientific data that pertains to teen sexual health.

Our friend Dr. Nanci Coppola runs Project Reach, which currently is working in the poorest neighborhoods of Yonkers, New York. She often recounts the story of a young man, who during a goal-setting exercise, told the class that his goal was to live until his twentieth birthday, the first man in his family to do so in a few generations. He went on to say that Dr. Coppola's *Healthy Respect* program gave him hope that he could reach that goal. A peer reviewed study published recently found that an expenditure of $1,000 on *Healthy Respect* prevents 13.67 teen pregnancies.

While it is difficult to be sure about all the causes of the steady decline in teen pregnancy, it is clear that SRA programs are contributing to the progress. According to CDC [Centers for Disease Control and Prevention] data from the *National Survey of Family Growth*, the proportion of teenagers ages fifteen to seventeen who have never had sex has risen from 62 percent in 1995 to 73 percent in 2006–2010 among females, and from 56.9 percent to 72 percent for males. These are very substantial gains during the period in which SRA programs have been widely implemented.

Clearing Up Misinformation Surrounding Abstinence Education

There is, of course, always room for improvement. To that end, the National Abstinence Education Association (NAEA), where we serve as president and board member respectively, as the professional association for SRA abstinence education, believes it is important that every provider have a foundational understanding of the theoretical and educational basis and science behind the SRA approach.

SRA abstinence education is a public health intervention, based on science and evidence, using sound pedagogy and methodology, to deliver a sound health message to young men and women.

We believe they should understand the social science research that corresponds to the overwhelming benefits of sexual delay. We think SRA educators should recognize effective teaching methods and have access to the most up-to-date scientific data that pertains to teen sexual health. For that reason, NAEA encourages each provider to earn Sexual Risk Avoidance Specialist professional credentials, through a rigorous certification program.

It is also important, in light of the criticism from religious conservatives, to note what SRA abstinence education is not. It is not a program of religious instruction. We strongly encourage parents to teach their children according to their religious and moral convictions on matters of sex, marriage, and childbearing. And we strongly encourage religious organizations to promote their views on these matters. Alexander and other bloggers who have been commenting on this controversy are partial to a Catholic approach based on John Paul II's *Theology of the Body* [Pope John Paul II was leader of the Catholic Church from 1978–2005]. More power to them. But SRA abstinence education is not, cannot be, and should not be a program in the *Theology of the Body*.

SRA abstinence education is a public health intervention, based on science and evidence, using sound pedagogy and methodology, to deliver a sound health message to young men and women, primarily in school settings. At that, it is very good and getting better.

We invite critics to take a closer look at the great progress made in the field and at the growing body of evidence showing the effectiveness of the approach. An honest look at the mountains of misinformation reveals unfounded and exaggerated charges with very little basis in reality.

Each teen deserves the caring encouragement to wait for sex. They deserve to have their dignity affirmed, along with their lack of culpability if they were sexually victimized. And those who chose to have sex too soon deserve to be reminded that their past does not need to predict their future. Each day begins with a new opportunity to make healthier decisions. There are never any "sloppy seconds," or leftover lives in our view, only precious young people who need our encouragement for health and well-being as they walk toward adulthood.

10

Sex Education Should Be Taught at Home as Well as in Schools

AVERT

AVERT is an international HIV and AIDS charity based in the United Kingdom working to avert HIV and AIDS worldwide through education, treatment, and care. AVERT was previously known as the AIDS Education and Research Trust.

Young people have the right to information about matters that affect them, and that includes information about sexuality and protecting themselves from unintended pregnancies and sexually transmitted diseases. While schools are an effective setting to provide existing knowledge and medically accurate information for young people, parents are in an ideal position to begin teaching children about their bodies and their sexuality at a very young age. Furthermore, parents and caregivers are able to engage in confidential conversations about sexuality with their children as specific questions and experiences arise.

Sex education ('sex ed'), which is sometimes called sexuality education or sex and relationships education, is the process of acquiring information and forming attitudes and beliefs about sex, sexual identity, relationships and intimacy. Sex education is also about developing young people's skills so that they make informed choices about their behaviour, and feel confident and competent about acting on these choices.

It is widely accepted that young people have a right to sex education. This is because it is a means by which they are helped to protect themselves against abuse, exploitation, unintended pregnancies, sexually transmitted diseases and HIV and AIDS. It is also argued that providing sex education helps to meet young people's rights to information about matters that affect them, their right to have their needs met and to help them enjoy their sexuality and the relationships that they form.

What Are the Aims of Sex Education?

Sex education aims to reduce the risks of potentially negative outcomes from sexual behaviour, such as unwanted or unplanned pregnancies and infection with sexually transmitted diseases including HIV.

Sex education also aims to contribute to young people's positive experience of their sexuality by enhancing the quality of their relationships and their ability to make informed decisions over their lifetime. Sex education that works, by which we mean that it is effective, is sex education that contributes to both these aims thus helping young people to be safe and enjoy their sexuality.

If sex education is going to be effective it needs to include opportunities for young people to develop skills, as it can be hard for them to act on the basis of only having information. The skills young people develop as part of sex education are linked to more general life-skills. Being able to communicate, listen, negotiate with others, ask for and identify sources of help and advice, are useful life-skills which can be applied to sexual relationships.

Effective sex education develops young people's skills in negotiation, decision-making, assertion and listening. Other important skills include being able to recognise pressures from other people and to resist them, dealing with and challenging prejudice and being able to seek help from adults—including parents, carers [caregivers] and professionals—through the family, community and health and welfare services.

Sex education that works also helps equip young people with the skills to be able to differentiate between accurate and inaccurate information, and to discuss a range of moral and social issues and perspectives on sex and sexuality, including different cultural attitudes and sensitive issues like sexuality, abortion and contraception. . . .

> *Effective sex education . . . provides young people with an opportunity to explore the reasons why people have sex.*

Attempts to impose narrow moralistic views about sex and sexuality on young people through sex education have failed. Rather than trying to deter or frighten young people away from having sex, effective sex education includes work on attitudes and beliefs, coupled with skills development, that enables young people to choose whether or not to have a sexual relationship taking into account the potential risks of any sexual activity.

Effective sex education also provides young people with an opportunity to explore the reasons why people have sex and to think about how it involves emotions, respect for oneself and other people and their feelings, decisions and bodies. Young people should have the chance to explore gender differences and how ethnicity and sexuality can influence people's feelings and options. They should be able to decide for themselves what the positive qualities of relationships are. It is important that they understand how bullying, stereotyping, abuse and exploitation can negatively influence relationships.

What Information Should Be Given to Young People?

Young people get information about sex and sexuality from a wide range of sources including each other, through the media including advertising, television and magazines, as well as leaflets, books and websites which are intended to be sources of information about sex and sexuality. Some of this will be accurate and some inaccurate.

Providing information through sex education is therefore about finding out what young people already know and adding to their existing knowledge and correcting any misinformation they may have. For example, young people may have heard that condoms are not effective against HIV or that there is a cure for AIDS. It is important to provide information which corrects mistaken beliefs. Without correct information young people can put themselves at greater risk.

It is important for sex education to begin at a young age and also that it is sustained.

Information is also important as the basis on which young people can develop well-informed attitudes and views about sex and sexuality. Young people need to have information on all the following topics:

- Sexual development & reproduction—the physical and emotional changes associated with puberty and sexual reproduction, including fertilisation and conception, as well as sexually transmitted diseases and HIV.

- Contraception & birth control—what contraceptives there are, how they work, how people use them, how they decide what to use or not, and how they can be obtained.

- Relationships—what kinds of relationships there are, love and commitment, marriage and partnership and the law relating to sexual behaviour and relationships as well as the range of religious and cultural views on sex and sexuality and sexual diversity.

In addition, young people should be provided with information about abortion, sexuality, and confidentiality, as well as about the range of sources of advice and support that is available in the community and nationally.

When Should Sex Education Start?

Sex education that works starts early, before young people reach puberty, and before they have developed established patterns of behaviour. The precise age at which information should be provided depends on the physical, emotional and intellectual development of the young people as well as their level of understanding. What is covered and also how, depends on who is providing the sex education, when they are providing it, and in what context, as well as what the individual young person wants to know about.

Parents can fulfill a particularly important role in providing information and opportunities to discuss things as they arise.

It is important for sex education to begin at a young age and also that it is sustained. Giving young people basic information from an early age provides the foundation on which more complex knowledge is built up over time. For example, when they are very young, children can be informed about how people grow and change over time, and how babies become children and then adults, and this provides the basis on which they understand more detailed information about puberty provided in the pre-teenage years. They can also when they are young, be provided with information about viruses and germs that attack the body. This provides the basis for talking to them later about infections that can be caught through sexual contact.

Some people are concerned that providing information about sex and sexuality arouses curiosity and can lead to sexual experimentation. However, in a review of 48 studies of comprehensive sex and STD/HIV education programmes in US schools, there was found to be strong evidence that such programmes did not increase sexual activity. Some of them reduced sexual activity, or increased rates of condom use or other contraceptives, or both. It is important to remember that young people can store up information provided at any time, for a time when they need it later on.

Sometimes it can be difficult for adults to know when to raise issues, but the important thing is to maintain an open relationship with children which provides them with opportunities to ask questions when they have them. Parents and carers can also be proactive and engage young people in discussions about sex sexuality and relationships. Naturally, many parents and their children feel embarrassed about talking about some aspects of sex and sexuality. Viewing sex education as an on-going conversation about values, attitudes and issues as well as providing facts can be helpful.

There is evidence that positive parent-child communication about sexual matters can lead to greater condom use among young men and a lower rate of teenage conception among young women.

The best basis to proceed on is a sound relationship in which a young person feels able to ask a question or raise an issue if they feel they need to. It has been shown that in countries like The Netherlands, where many families regard it as an important responsibility to talk openly with children about sex and sexuality, this contributes to greater cultural openness about sex and sexuality and improved sexual health among young people.

The role of many parents and carers as sex educators changes as young people get older and are provided with more opportunities to receive formal sex education through schools and community-settings. However, it doesn't get any less important. Because sex education in school tends to take place in blocks of time, it can't always address issues relevant to young people at a particular time, and parents can fulfill a particularly important role in providing information and opportunities to discuss things as they arise.

Who Should Provide Sex Education?

Sex education can take place in a variety of settings, both in and out of school. In these different contexts, different people have the opportunity and responsibility to provide sex education for young people.

At home, young people can easily have one-to-one discussions with parents or carers which focus on specific issues, questions or concerns. They can have a dialogue about their attitudes and views. Sex education at home also tends to take place over a long time, and involve lots of short interactions between parents and children.

There may be times when young people seem reluctant to talk, but it is important not to interpret any diffidence as meaning that there is nothing left to talk about. As young people get older advantage can be taken of opportunities provided by things seen on television for example, as an opportunity to initiate conversation.

It is also important not to defer dealing with a question or issue for too long as it can suggest that you are unwilling to talk about it. There is evidence that positive parent-child communication about sexual matters can lead to greater condom use among young men and a lower rate of teenage conception among young women.

In school the interaction between the teacher and young people takes a different form and is often provided in organised blocks of lessons. It is not as well suited to advising the individual as it is to providing information from an impartial point of view.

The most effective sex education acknowledges the different contributions each setting can make. School programmes which involve parents, notifying them what is being taught and when, can support the initiation of dialogue at home. Parents and schools both need to engage with young people about the messages that they get from the media, and give them opportunities for discussion. . . .

Parents are best placed in relation to young people to provide continuity of individual support and education starting from early in their lives.

School-based sex education can be an important and effective way of enhancing young people's knowledge, attitudes and behaviour. There is widespread agreement that formal education should include sex education and what works has been well-researched. Evidence suggests that effective school programmes will include the following elements:

- A focus on reducing specific risky behaviours

- A basis in theories which explain what influences people's sexual choices and behaviour

- A clear, and continuously reinforced message about sexual behavior and risk reduction

- Providing accurate information about the risks associated with sexual activity, about contraception and birth control, and about methods of avoiding or deferring intercourse

- Dealing with peer and other social pressures on young people; providing opportunities to practice communication, negotiation and assertion skills.

- Uses a variety of approaches to teaching and learning that involve and engage young people and help them to personalise the information

- Uses approaches to teaching and learning which are appropriate to young people's age, experience and cultural background

- Is provided by people who believe in what they are saying and have access to support in the form of training or consultation with other sex educators

Formal programmes with all these elements have been shown to increase young people's levels of knowledge about sex and sexuality, put back the average age at which they first have sexual intercourse and decrease risk when they do have sex. . . .

How Can Various Sex Educators Work Together?

Providing effective sex education can seem daunting because it means tackling potentially sensitive issues and involving a variety of people—parents, schools, community groups and health service providers. However, because sex education comprises many individual activities, which take place across a wide range of settings and periods of time, there are lots of opportunities to contribute.

The nature of a person's contribution depends on their relationship, role and expertise in relation to young people. For example, parents are best placed in relation to young people to provide continuity of individual support and education starting from early in their lives.

School-based education programmes are particularly good at providing information and opportunities for skills development and attitude clarification in more formal ways, through lessons within a curriculum. Community-based projects provide opportunities for young people to access advice and information in less formal ways.

Sexual health and other health and welfare services can provide access to specific information, support and advice. Sex education through the mass media, often supported by local, regional or national government and non-governmental agencies and departments, can help to raise public awareness of sex health issues.

Further development of sex education partly depends on joining up these elements in a coherent way to meet the needs of young people. There is also a need to pay more attention to the needs of specific groups of young people like young parents, young lesbian, gay and bisexual people, as well as those who may be out of touch with services and schools, and socially vulnerable, like young refugees and asylum-seekers, young people in care, young people in prisons, and also those living on the street.

The circumstances and context available to parents and other sex educators are different from place to place. Practical or political realities in a particular country may limit people's ability to provide young people with comprehensive sex education combining all the elements in the best way possible. But the basic principles outlined here apply everywhere. By making our own contribution and valuing that made by others, and by being guided by these principles, we can provide more sex education that works and improve the support we offer to young people.

11

Abstinence Programs Isolate LGBTQ Youth

Sexuality Information and Education Council of the United States

The Sexuality Information and Education Council of the United States (SIECUS) is a clearinghouse for information on sexuality, with a special interest in sex education.

As a minority population in schools nationwide, lesbian, gay, bisexual, transgender, and questioning (LGBTQ) youth experience verbal, physical, and sexual harassment every day and are the target of homophobic remarks from both students and staff. Abstinence education programs perpetuate such mistreatment by either promoting a clear bias against homosexuality or simply omitting the subject of sexual orientation in the curriculum. As a result, abstinence education programs commit a disservice to not only LGBTQ youth but to all youth.

Three percent of high school students describe themselves as lesbian, gay, or bisexual, and over five percent report they are either lesbian, gay, bisexual, or have had sexual experiences with individuals of the same sex. As a minority population in schools across the country, LGBTQ [lesbian, gay, bisexual, transgender, and questioning] youth commonly experience high rates of discrimination and harassment, yet are often not protected under school policy. And even though most parents favor teaching about sexual orientation in schools, most sexuality education programs do not cover this topic and abstinence-only-until-marriage programs merely further negative sentiment toward these students. As a result, LGBTQ youth are more vulnerable to a variety of harmful behaviors, including skipping school and attempting suicide, than their heterosexual peers.

To overcome bias against LGBTQ youth, sexuality education programs must consider and include sexual orientation.

LGBTQ Youth Are More Vulnerable to Harmful Behavior

Homophobic remarks and harassment, lack of protection at school, and negative messages from abstinence-only-until-marriage programs all contribute to making LGBTQ youth more at risk for harmful behavior than heterosexual students.

- Over twice as many lesbian, gay, and bisexual students (19%) report being threatened or injured with a weapon at their public high school during the year than heterosexual students (8%).

- Lesbian, gay, and bisexual students (16%) are twice as likely to have skipped school in the last month for safety concerns as other students (8%).

- Attempted suicide rates are over four times higher for lesbian, gay, and bisexual students; 33% report that they attempted to commit suicide during the past year, compared with only 9% of all other students.

LGBTQ Youth Experience Discrimination and Harassment at School

LGBTQ youth often hear homophobic remarks from both students and staff. Many of these students are verbally, physically, and sexually harassed because of their sexual orientation, and as a result, report feeling unsafe at school.

- 92% of lesbian, gay, bisexual, and transgender students in middle and high school report that they frequently or often hear homophobic remarks, such as "faggot," "dyke," or the expression "that's so gay" from their peers. Almost one in five of these students heard homophobic remarks from faculty or staff at their school.

- 84% of middle and high school aged lesbian, gay, bisexual, and transgender youth say they are verbally harassed at school, including name calling or threats, because of their sexual orientation.

- 65% of these students report having been sexually harassed over the past school year, including sexual remarks or touching, because of their sexual orientation.

- 39% report having been physical harassed, including being shoved or pushed at school, because of their sexual orientation.

- 64% of lesbian, gay, bisexual, and transgender students in middle and high schools say they feel unsafe at school.

- Lesbian, gay, bisexual, and transgender high school seniors who have experienced higher frequencies of verbal harassment at school (13%) are more likely to report they do not plan to attend college than lesbian, gay, bisexual, or transgender seniors who have never or rarely experienced verbal harassment (7%).

Most LGBTQ Students Are Not Protected from Discrimination and Harassment

Most state policies do not provide protection for LGBTQ students. Currently, only eight states and the District of Columbia legally protect students based on their sexual orientation. And, six states actually prohibit "advocacy of homosexuality" at school.

- Over 75% of students in the United States attend schools in states where sexual orientation and identity are not protected classes under the law as religion, race and national origin are under federal law.

- Teachers cannot portray homosexuality as an acceptable lifestyle in Arizona, Alabama, Mississippi, South Carolina, Texas, and Utah. In some of these states, students were reminded that homosexual conduct is a criminal offense despite the fact that in 2003 the United States Supreme Court ruled, in *Lawrence v. Texas,* that such laws were unconstitutional.

Parents Support Teaching About Sexual Orientation at Schools

Three out of four parents feel comfortable speaking to their children about homosexuality, but are unlikely to raise this topic on their own. To overcome bias against LGBTQ youth, sexuality education programs must consider and include sexual orientation.

- 79% of parents want their children to learn about sexual orientation in sexuality education classes at school.

- 67% of parents believe their children should be taught that gay people are just like other people.

Abstinence-Only-Until-Marriage Programs Further Isolate LGBTQ Youth

Abstinence-only-until-marriage curricula ignore the needs of LGBTQ youth. They either omit sexual orientation completely or show clear bias against homosexuality and as such are clearly not appropriate for American schools.

- Abstinence-only-until-marriage curricula ignore LGBTQ youth.

For example, *Choosing The Best* curriculum teaches students "one of the major purposes of dating is to understand members of the opposite sex."

- Abstinence-only-until-marriage curricula show clear bias against homosexuality.

CLUE 2000 equates homosexuality with clearly immoral and illegal behavior, such as incest or pedophilia: "Among [researcher Alfred C.] Kinsey's most outrageous and damaging claims are the beliefs that pedophilia, homosexuality, incest, and adult-child sex are normal."

Sexual Orientation and Identity Defined

The understanding and identification of one's sexual orientation may change over the course of a person's life. And while many people identify themselves as having a certain sexual orientation based on whom they are attracted to or fall in love with, this is not always the case. For example, there are some people who have sexual thoughts and experiences with people of the same gender, but do not consider themselves to be gay, lesbian, or bisexual. And, there are people who have sexual thoughts and experiences with people of the other gender but do not consider themselves to be heterosexual.

- Heterosexual (or straight) refers to a person who is attracted to and falls in love with someone of *another* gender, and homosexual (or gay man or lesbian woman) refers to a person who is attracted to and falls in love with someone of the *same* gender. A bisexual person is attracted to and falls in love with someone of *another or the same* gender.

- Questioning refers to a person who is *unsure* of his/her sexual orientation.

- Transgender refers to individuals whose internal feelings of being male or female differ from the sexual anatomy they were born with. Transgender refers to *gender identity*, not sexual orientation.

12

Sex Education Policy Needs to Be Revised

Andrew Jenkins

Andrew Jenkins, a social justice activist, is a contributing author to RH Reality Check, *an online news site dedicated to reproductive health and rights, and is a field associate at Choice USA, a national pro-choice organization.*

Sex education for youth today is based on fear—fear of pregnancy, fear of sexually transmitted diseases, fear of sexual assault, fear of any adverse consequences that could result from sexual activity. Young people deserve better. In fact, it is a fundamental right for young people to receive honest and comprehensive information, which includes the positive and fulfilling aspects about sex and sexuality. If politicians, institutions, and even parents continue to perpetuate the culture of sexual fear and shame, it is left to young people themselves to demand sex education that prioritizes their health and well-being.

Knowledge is power.

I mean that in the most cliché way possible. Without knowledge, agency and self-determination become meaningless fragments of our imagination. Something that we desperately wish for but can't quite grab onto. This is especially true when it comes to young people.

Growing up in the United States is like playing a foucauldian [philosophy that power can shape knowledge] game of discipline and punish. Disciplined by a morally bankrupt narrative about sex and sexuality and then punished for daring to question it.

Sex Education Should Not Be Based on Fear

I guess we shouldn't be all that surprised. When young people are subjugated and disenfranchised, systems of power thrive. When we're alienated from our bodies and fearful of our sexuality, we lack the resources and agency necessary to become responsible agents of social and political change. Suffice it to say; those in power have a vested interest in dislocating the nation's youth from real sex education.

For young people, sexuality is undoubtedly the most politicized site of social control. Parents fear it. Politicians debate over it. Scientists study it. Intellectuals theorize over it. Everyone is talking about it; yet, no one is talking to young people.

The pseudo-scientific narrative about youth sexuality is plagued with fear mongering and sensationalism.

It doesn't take a semester of reading Michel Foucault [French philosopher who explored how power shapes knowledge] to understand that sexuality is an important site of power. Young people know very intimately the role that sex and sexuality play in our daily lives and we know the detrimental consequences that a sex-phobic culture has on our futures. We're experiencing it first-hand. Attacks on birth control. Abstinence-only programs. Sexist gender roles. Compulsive heterosexuality and homophobia. Misinformation about abortion. Age restrictions on emergency contraception. Sexual assault. Negative representations of teen motherhood. Public health initiatives that securitize youth sexuality.

We have experienced the damaging effects of a culture that stigmatizes sexuality and shames young people for exploring our own bodies. And we're sick of it.

The pseudo-scientific narrative about youth sexuality is plagued with fear mongering and sensationalism. Between the bogus sexting panic, and the fear-based rhetoric used to justify the recent HHS ruling [in 2011, the US Department of Health and Human Services (HHS) prohibited over-the-counter sales of the "morning after pill" to girls under the age of 17] on emergency contraception, it is very clear that the moral panic over teen sexuality is very much alive and kicking. Even organizations and politicians sensible enough to support comprehensive sex education are still situating the issue within a broader security paradigm. They want us to educate young people about the ramifications of sex because they don't want us engaging in sexual relationships to begin with. They've been duped by the myth of the teen pregnancy epidemic.

Don't get me wrong. Unintended pregnancy rates in the United States are high. Sexually transmitted infections are rampant. But this isn't only affecting young people and it certainly isn't because we're irresponsible and incapable of making good choices. It's because no one believes in our ability to be good decision-makers. Whether they're shoving abstinence-only programs down our throat, or they're giving us access to sex education rooted in fear tactics, the message is still the same: that sex among young people is a serious threat to the morality and security of the nation.

That's the interesting thing about sex education. It's about much more than just the birds and the bees. It's about power. Power derived from knowledge. The power to shape our own destiny.

Sex Education Should Include Positive Aspects of Sexuality

Many of the people advocating for comprehensive sex education at the local, state and federal level treat youth sexuality as a crisis to be averted. They're so caught up with trying to rally support for the cause with alarming statistics and fear-based rhetoric that they lose site of the real problem. Young people don't just need to know about the potential ramifications of sex. We need to know what the benefits of a healthy, consensual, and autonomous sex life look like. We need the decision-making power necessary to navigate this difficult terrain and we need to know that after given the facts about sex and sexuality, we're going to be trusted to make our own choices.

Not a single person, political figure, or institution knows what young people need more than young people themselves.

The radical shift from an abstinence-only framework to a comprehensive one loses its transformative potential if our previous generation is still setting the rules. This is why we desperately need a youth-centered and youth-led struggle for comprehensive sex education. Young people have to lead the way in shaping sex education policy. Otherwise, we're destined to replicate the same morally bankrupt narrative that youth sexuality is an epidemic of global proportions.

We have to change the very way we think about sex and sexuality. Instead of treating it as a social parasite, we should embrace it. We need to teach young folks that when treated with maturity, reciprocity and awareness, sex can be an exciting, fulfilling, and even empowering aspect of our lives. Learning to love our bodies is one of the most radical things we can do in a culture sustained by oppressive power structures. However, as long as we're taught to feel shameful about our bodies, and denied the right to sex-positive comprehensive sex education, we're doomed to replicate the very systems of domination that thrive on our ignorance and complacency.

Young People Should Demand Honest Sex Education

Not a single person, political figure, or institution knows what young people need more than young people themselves. We understand the unique differences in the way our generation feels about sex and sexuality and as a result, we need to be the ones shaping a new discourse. And that's exactly what we're doing.

We need politicians who are more than just apathetic on the issue of sex education. We need pro-active advocates that are unwavering in their commitment to our health and well-being.

Young people are telling their stories and demanding that Congress replace failed abstinence-only programs with comprehensive sex education. We're asking our Senators and Representatives to support the Real Education for Healthy Youth Act, an effort that prioritizes young people. Not to mention the first piece of legislation to ever identify comprehensive sex education as a fundamental right.

Thanks to the courage and creativity of young people, we've seen the federal government fund comprehensive sex education for the first time in history. We've secured no-cost birth control for millions of women through the Affordable Care Act and we played a crucial role in protecting abortion and family planning from the onslaught of radical anti-choice zealots in Congress. We've developed innovative ways to educate our peers through services like sexetc.org. Clearly, we have a great deal of legislative and cultural advances to be proud of.

But the momentum can't stop here. . . .

We can make the message clear that if our elected officials aren't willing to stand up for us—and defend our basic right to honest and accurate information about sex and sexuality—we're not going to show up for them. It's as simple as that. We need politicians who are more than just apathetic on the issue of sex education. We need pro-active advocates that are unwavering in their commitment to our health and well-being.

Proponents that are willing to stand up for young people when push comes to shove and our livelihood is on the chopping block.

It may be difficult to articulate a new vision for change without couching it in the same flawed security logic and fear rhetoric that undermines young people in the first place. But we have no other choice.

We have to draw a line in the sand and make it clear that if our elected officials aren't willing to stand up for our health, they'll have to answer to the most powerful electoral force in the country: young people.

13

Parents Should Be More Open and Honest About Teenage Sexuality

Amanda Marcotte

Amanda Marcotte is an American journalist best known for her writing on feminism and politics. She is the author of the book Get Opinionated *and contributes to* Slate, The Guardian, *and* RH Reality Check.

Much like past generations, many parents of today feel uncomfortable with the concept of their teenagers having sex. Such discomfort is dangerous as it can discourage children from turning to their parents for information and advice regarding relationships, contraception usage, and sexually transmitted diseases. If parents would reflect back on their own experience as a teenager growing up amidst shame- and fear-based attitudes about sexuality, perhaps they would become more honest and respectful of their own children's sexuality. And everyone would benefit in the long run.

A year after the [2008] election that catapulted her to fame, Sarah Palin [Republican nominee for vice president]—mother of the most famous [unwed] teenage mother [Bristol Palin] in the country—swore to Barbara Walters [broadcast journalist] that she had no idea that her daughter was having sex when she announced her pregnancy. Many Americans, including myself, scoffed, figuring she was simply spouting something that's more politically convenient than likely. Levi Johnston's [baby's father] insinuations that the Palin family knew felt more true; how can parents not figure it out when their teenagers are sexually active?

Many Parents Are Unaware of Children's Sexual Activity

Turns out that perhaps Sarah Palin's purported ignorance might not be as unusual as it initially seems. A recent CBS poll demonstrated that only 22 percent of parents think their teenaged children are sexually active. Unfortunately for them, 46 percent of teenagers are actually sexually active, which means that more than half the kids having sex are managing to hide that fact from their parents.

The very people who thought they were right to have sex as teenagers then grow up to pass on denial and shame to their own kids.

"So what?" you might ask. It's a good question. After all, one's sexual activity is a private matter, and even though teenagers may live under their parents' house, they still have a right to a private life. Many parents accept this, which is probably why teenagers are able to hide their sexual activity—their parents respect their privacy and don't root through their email, cell phones, or even perform the old-fashioned underwear drawer search. Perhaps one could even argue that this level of privacy encourages contraception usage. It's true that kids who are ready to have sex but not ready to share that with their parents are probably going to be more likely to use contraception if they can do so without their parents finding out.

But despite this, we should still be concerned that so many American parents are living in denial about teenage sexuality.

In the moment, denial might be the best of all bad choices, but we should understand that denial is a symptom of a larger problem of shame and fear about sexuality, especially teenage sexuality. And shame and fear about sexuality are linked to sexual irresponsibility that then leads to teenage pregnancy and STD [sexually transmitted disease] transmission.

An Attitude Adjustment for Parents Is Necessary

Don't take my word for it. Look at the evidence. In January 2008, I reported on a study that compared attitudes towards teenage sexuality in Holland and the U.S. Holland is of particular interest, because while their teenagers have sex at the same rates and ages as ours, their STD transmission rate and teenage pregnancy rate are much lower. What researchers found should have been earth-shattering, even as it seems sort of obvious in retrospect. It was something very simple: Dutch parents were more likely to respect teenage sexuality and treat teenage love affairs as the real deal, instead of some sick thing for teenagers to avoid. In fact, Dutch parents were way likelier to allow teenaged children to have sleepovers with their romantic partners. Not living in denial about their kids' sexual activity, not like American parents.

I said it then and I'll say it now—young people show a tendency to rise to the expectations we put on them, and this research shows it. If you respect young people's sexuality and expect them to behave like responsible adults about it, you will get far more young people actually taking health precautions and behaving respectfully. If you treat sex like it's a dirty secret that must be denied and hidden, kids will be more prone to have furtive sexual encounters, without taking as much time and energy to consider contraception and basics like vetting their partners for good will and respect.

The irony in all this is that most of us had sex as teenagers, and most of us went to great lengths to conceal this fact from our parents. You'd think we would have learned the dangers of shame and denial, from the unfortunate lack of pre-paredness (thinking you can't have condoms on hand, because what if they find out!) to the gaping lack of guidance from your elders on how to conduct relationships, due to the fact that you were hiding the exact nature of those relationships. We were right to fear judgment in our puritanical society, but what's baffling to me is how the very people who thought they were right to have sex as teenagers then grow up to pass on denial and shame to their own kids.

A Generation Gap Is Not Inevitable

It shouldn't surprise me, though. A lot of us repeat the mis-takes of our parents because we don't realize there are other options. This is particularly true of sex. The gulf of knowledge and understanding between generations about sex persists be-cause we believe that because it's always been there (as far as we know), it's just the way things are and always will be. But as the Dutch example shows, there's nothing inevitable about the wall of silence between generations. There can be more openness about sexuality, and everyone would benefit from a little more honesty.

Obviously, I'm not talking about sharing the details. We don't need to know our parents' proclivities or frequency in order to grasp that they do have sex, proving that one can know that something's happening without having to know all the gross out details. All I propose is that the same sort of "we know of it, but we don't need to know all the details" attitude that is extended towards adult relatives, friends, and even be-tween sexually active teenagers themselves can be extended to teenagers from the adult authority figures in their lives, espe-cially their parents. And even though teenagers often feel the urge to shut their parents out of their business, knowing that their parents know and don't judge leaves the door open for teenagers to come to their parents for help if they need it.

And you don't get that if denial and shame are the stan-dards.

Organizations to Contact

The editors have compiled the following list of organizations concerned with the issues debated in this book. The descriptions are derived from materials provided by the organizations. All have publications or information available for interested readers. The list was compiled on the date of publication of the present volume; the information here may change. Be aware that many organizations take several weeks or longer to respond to inquiries, so allow as much time as possible.

Advocates for Youth
2000 M St. NW, Suite 750, Washington, DC 20036
(202) 419-3420 • fax: (202) 419-1448
e-mail: information@advocatesforyouth.org
website: www.advocatesforyouth.org

Advocates for Youth believes young people have the right to accurate and complete sexual health information to enable them to make healthy decisions about sexuality, and about confidential reproductive and sexual health services. The organization publishes fact sheets, policy briefs, and brochures on adolescent behavior and sexuality including "Abstinence-Only-Until-Marriage Programs: Ineffective, Unethical, and Poor Public Health" and "Comprehensive Sex Education and Academic Success."

Alliance Defending Freedom (ADF)
15100 N 90th St., Scottsdale, AZ 85260
(800) 835-5233 • fax: (480) 444-0025
website: www.alliancedefendingfreedom.org

Alliance Defending Freedom (ADF) is a legal alliance defending the right to hear and speak about Christian beliefs through the legal defense and advocacy of religious freedom, the sanctity of human life, and traditional family values. They believe that it is the responsibility of parents to educate their children about sex and defend the right of parents to opt their children out of explicit sex education classes. In addition to position statements supporting these rights, the ADF website functions as a clearinghouse of news regarding sex education.

American Civil Liberties Union (ACLU)
125 Broad St., 18th Floor, New York, NY   10004
(212) 549-2500
website: www.aclu.org

The American Civil Liberties Union (ACLU) is a national organization that works to defend American's civil rights as guaranteed by the US Constitution. It opposes federal funding for abstinence-only sex education arguing that it violates the civil rights and the freedom of speech of students and teachers. Among the ACLU's numerous publications are "God and Abstinence," "ACLU Comments to Community-Based Abstinence Education Performance Progress Report," and "Abstinence-Only Education Fact Sheet."

American Federation of Teachers (AFT)
555 New Jersey Ave. NW, Washington, DC   20001
(202) 879-4400
website: www.aft.org

The American Federation of Teachers (AFT), an affiliated international union of the AFL-CIO, a federation of labor organizations, was founded in 1916 to represent the economic, social, and professional interests of classroom teachers. It now includes paraprofessionals and school-related personnel; local, state and federal employees; higher education faculty and staff; and nurses and other healthcare professionals. The ATF supports comprehensive sex education and strongly argues against abstinence-only curricula as is expressed in their position statement, "Support for Reproductive Rights." Its website provides links to news stories, reports on key issues, e-mail newsletters on topics such as early childhood education, videos, and press releases.

Family Research Council (FRC)

801 G St. NW, Washington, DC   20001

(202) 393-2100 • fax: (202) 393-2134

website: www.frc.org

A nonprofit organization founded in 1983, the Family Research Council (FRC) is a conservative Christian group and
lobbying organization. The FRC supports abstinence-until-
marriage sex education, where marriage between one man
and woman is promoted as the expected context for sexual
behaviors and as the best family structure for raising children.
The FRC further believes that abstinence education promotes
the optimal reproductive health, sexual health, and psychoso-
cial and societal outcomes. Its website publishes a blog and
provides links to insight papers including "Why Wait: The
Benefits of Abstinence Until Marriage," perspective papers including "Spending Too Little On Abstinence," and policy lec-
tures, such as "Why Isn't Anyone Telling Our Kids about the
Dangers of Casual Sex."

Focus on the Family (FOTF)

8605 Explorer Dr., Colorado Springs, CO   80920-1051

(800) 232-6459 • fax: (719) 548-5947

e-mail: pastors@fotf.org

website: www.focusonthefamily.com

Focus on the Family (FOTF), a nonprofit organization
founded in 1977, is a global Christian ministry dedicated to
building healthy marriages and to raising children according
to morals and values grounded in biblical principles. FOTF
supports abstinence-only sexual education and opposes di-
vorce, pre-marital sex, and Lesbian, Gay, Bisexual, and Transgender rights. The organization publishes videos; audio re-
cordings; magazines, such as *Thriving Family Magazine*; books,
such as *The Purity Code*; and articles, including "Why Wait for
Sex?" "Risk Factors for Premarital Sex," and "Making Decisions About Sex."

National Abstinence Education Association (NAEA)

2625 Cumberland Pkwy., Suite 200, Atlanta, GA   30339
(202) 248-5420 • fax: (866) 935-4850
e-mail: info@theNAEA.org
website: www.abstinenceassociation.org

Founded in 2006, the National Abstinence Education Association (NAEA) exists to serve, support, and represent individuals and organizations in the practice of abstinence education. As a nonprofit organization, NAEA is able to offer unique member services for abstinence education organizations, educators, and providers, including unlimited lobbying on behalf of abstinence education. Among their many statements in support of abstinence-only education is "Abstinence Education Cuts Teen Sex by 50%" and "STD Crisis Requires Priority on Prevention." NAEA's website also provides links to research and reports including "Sex Risk Avoidance SRA Abstinence Education and Gay Teens" and "Families Matter in Reducing Teen Sexual Activity."

National Association of State Boards of Education (NASBE)

2121 Crystal Dr., Suite 350, Arlington, VA   22202
(703) 684-4000 • fax: (703) 836-2313
website: www.nasbe.org

A nonprofit organization founded in 1958, the National Association of State Boards of Education (NASBE) works to strengthen state leadership in educational policymaking, promote excellence in the education of all students, advocate equality of access to educational opportunity, and assure continued citizen support for public education. NASBE is opposed to abstinence-only education and endorses comprehensive sex education. In addition to providing a clearinghouse of the latest news reports concerning sex education, NASBE's website offers an array of reports, periodicals, discussion guides, and the journal, *The State Education Standard*, discussing select education policy issues.

National Coalition Against Censorship (NCAC)
19 Fulton St., Suite 407, New York, NY   10038
(212) 807-6222
e-mail: ncac@ncac.org
website: www.ncac.org

Founded in 1974, the National Coalition Against Censorship (NCAC) is an alliance of fifty national nonprofit organizations, including literary, artistic, religious, educational, professional, labor, and civil liberties groups. United by a conviction that freedom of thought, inquiry, and expression is a fundamental human right and essential to a healthy democracy, the NCAC works to educate their members and the public at large about the dangers of censorship and how to oppose them. As expressed in several position statements, including "Fighting Abstinence-Only Education," the NCAC argues that abstinence-only education violates student and teacher rights to freedom of speech. The alliance publishes a quarterly newsletter, *NCAC Censorship News*, as well as articles and booklets, including "Abstinence-Only Education?"

National Education Association (NEA)
1201 16th St. NW, Washington, DC   20036-3290
(202) 833-4000 • fax: (202) 822-7974
website: www.nea.org

The National Education Association (NEA), the nation's largest professional employee organization, is a volunteer-based association of educators committed to advancing the cause of public education. The NEA argues that all students should have access to important health and sexuality information through appropriately established sex education programs in order to protect themselves and make informed decisions. Their website provides access to a number of position statements and research reports regarding sex education.

Pro-Choice Public Education Project (PEP)
PO Box 3952, New York, NY   10163
(212) 977-4266

e-mail: pep@protectchoice.org
website: www.protectchoice.org

The Pro-Choice Public Education Project (PEP) is dedicated to engaging and informing organizations, young women, and gender nonconforming young people about the critical issue of reproductive justice. The PEP is opposed to abstinence-only education and seeks to provide sex education that is comprehensive. In addition to its e-newsletter and many other resources for educators and young people, the PEP website serves as a clearinghouse for information regarding sex education and female sexuality.

Rethinking Schools

1001 E Keefe Ave., Milwaukee, WI   53212
(414) 964-9646 • fax: (414) 964-7220
e-mail: office@rethinkingschools.org
website: www.rethinkingschools.org

Rethinking Schools began as a local effort in Milwaukee, Wisconsin, to address problems such as basal readers, standardized testing, and textbook-dominated curricula. Since its founding in 1986, it has grown into a nationally prominent publisher of educational materials, with subscribers in all fifty states, all ten Canadian provinces, and many other countries. Rethinking Schools maintains an extensive collection of information regarding sex education, including a quarterly magazine, *Rethinking Schools—The Magazine,* and articles such as "Let's Talk about Sex: Why Aren't We Telling Kids the Full Story?" and "Preaching Ain't Teaching: Sex Education and America's New Puritans."

Sexuality Information and Education Council of the United States (SIECUS)

90 John St., Suite 402, New York, NY   10038
(212) 819-9770 • fax: (212) 819-9776
e-mail: mrodriguez@siecus.org
website: www.siecus.org

Founded in 1964, the Sexuality Information and Education Council of the United States (SIECUS) provides education and information about sexuality and sexual and reproductive health. SIECUS advocates for the right of all people to have access to accurate information, comprehensive education about sexuality, and sexual health services. In addition to providing a sex education library on their main website, SIECUS publishes position statements and special reports, such as "Legalized Discrimination: The Rise of the Marriage-Promotion Industry and How Federally Funded Programs Discriminate Against Lesbian, Gay, Bisexual, and Transgender Youth and Families," and "It Gets Worse: A Revamped Federal Abstinence-Only Program Goes Extreme."

Bibliography

Books

Michael Bradley *When Things Get Crazy with Your Teen: The Why, the How, and What to Do Now.* New York: McGraw-Hill, 2009.

Vicki Courtney *Five Conversations You Must Have with Your Daughter.* Nashville, TN: B&H Publishing, 2008.

Alesha E. Doan and Jean Calterone Williams *The Politics of Virginity: Abstinence in Sex Education.* Westport, CT: Praeger, 2008.

Sinikka Elliott *Not My Kid: What Parents Believe About the Sex Lives of Their Teenagers.* New York: NYU Press, 2012.

Stephen Feinstein *Sexuality and Teens: What You Should Know About Sex, Abstinence, Birth Control, Pregnancy and STDs.* Berkeley Heights, NJ: Enslow Publishers, 2009.

Robie H. Harris *It's Perfectly Normal: Changing Bodies, Growing Up, Sex, and Sexual Health.* Somerville, MA: Candlewick Press, 2009.

Sharnice A. Jones *Success Before Sex.* Mantua, NJ: Success 1st, 2012.

Nancy Kendall *The Sex Education Debates.* Chicago: University of Chicago Press, 2012.

Michael Kimmel *Guyland: The Perilous World Where Boys Become Men.* New York: Harper Collins, 2008.

Alexandra M. Lord *Condom Nation: The US Government's Sex Education Campaign from World War I to the Internet.* Baltimore, MD: Johns Hopkins University Press, 2010.

Erica R. Meiners and Therese Quinn, eds. *Sexualities in Education.* New York: Peter Lang Publishing, 2012.

C.J. Pascoe *Dude, You're a Fag: Masculinity and Sexuality in High School.* Berkeley: University of California Press, 2011.

Martha Roper *Teen Relationships: Using Values & Choices to Teach Sex Education.* Chicago: Search Institute Press, 2011.

Amy T. Schalet *Not Under My Roof: Parents, Teens, and the Culture of Sex.* Chicago: University of Chicago Press, 2011.

Richard O. Stroub *Health Psychology.* New York: Worth Publishers, 2012.

R. Murray Thomas *Sex and the American Teenager: Seeing Through the Myths and Confronting the Issues.* Lanham, MD: Rowman and Littlefield Education, 2009.

Kris Vallotton   *Purity: The New Moral Revolution.* Shippensburg, PA: Destiny Image Publishing, 2008.

Periodicals and Internet Sources

Erin Anderssen   "Abstinence-Only Programs Can Delay Teen Sex," *Globe and Mail,* August 23, 2012.

Hannah Boen   "Study Shows More Young People Are Abstaining from Sex," *Abilene Reporter News,* March 4, 2011.

Katherine Bradley and Christine Kim   "The Case for Maintaining Abstinence Education Funding," The Heritage Foundation, July 24, 2009. www.heritage.org.

Doortje Braeken   "Sex Education: We Should Teach Young People About More than the Mechanics," *The Guardian,* May 24, 2012.

K.J. Dell'Antonia   "Should We Have National Standards for Sex Education?" *New York Times* blog, January 10, 2012. www .parenting.blogs.nytimes.com.

Dyersburg State Gazette   "Report: Parents Support Abstinence Education," November 6, 2012. www.stategazette.com.

Steven Ertelt   "Abstinence Programs Credited with Reducing Teen Birth Rates," LifeNews.com, November 18, 2011.

Simcha Fisher   "Is THIS What Abstinence-Only Education Looks Like?" *National Catholic Register*, May 24, 2012. www.ncregister.com.

Barb Flis and Becky Griesse   "It's Time to Talk to Your Kids About Sex," *RH Reality Check*, April 9, 2013. http://rhrealitycheck.org.

Jane Fonda   "Young People Need, Demand Sex Education," *RH Reality Check*, April 16, 2009. http://rhrealitycheck.org.

Rose Garrett   "Sex Ed 101: What Your Child May Not Be Learning in School," Education.com, July 5, 2013.

Great Schools   "The Birds and the Bees: What's the Status of Sex Ed?" 2009. www.greatschools.org.

Valerie Huber   "Who Supports Abstinence Education? Parents," *Washington Examiner*, October 17, 2012.

Martha Kempner   "Dissecting the Outrageous, Inaccurate Claims Made at a High School Abstinence-Only Presention," *RH Reality Check*, July 18, 2013. http://rhrealitycheck.org.

Martha Kempner   "Parents and Teens Are Talking About Sex. They're Just Not Having the Same Conversation," *RH Reality Check*, October 10, 2012. http://rhrealitycheck.org.

Patrick Malone and Monica Rodriguez
"Comprehensive Sex Education vs. Abstinence-Only-Until-Marriage Programs," *Human Rights Magazine*, Spring 2011. www.americanbar.org.

Jenelle Marie
"How Abstinence-Only Ed Is Driving Up STD Rates," TakePart, April 3, 2013. www.takepart.com.

Jeannette Moninger
"How to Have the Sex Talk with Your Teen," *Family Circle*, November 2012.

Abigail Muldoon
"Why Christians Should Give Up Abstinence-Only Sex Education," ChicagoNow, May 10, 2013. www.chicagonow.com.

Scott Phelps
"Kids Don't Need Explicit Sex Ed," *Chicago Sun Times*, April 10, 2013.

Anna Quindlen
"Let's Talk About Sex," *Newsweek*, March 16, 2009.

Darshak Sanghavi
"Why Have Teen Pregnancy Rates Dropped?" *Slate*, July 31, 2012. www.slate.com.

Lisa Schencker
"Should Parents Get Sex Ed Training? Lawmakers Not Sure," *The Salt Lake Tribune*, October 18, 2012.

Emily Sellers
"A Sex Ed Reality Check," *The Dartmouth*, November 12, 2012.

Melanie Smollin
"Should Sex Ed Classes Be Mandatory?" TakePart, August 22, 2011. www.takepart.com.

Kate Stables   "The Joy of Sex Education," *Sight and Sound*, May 2009.

M.J. Stephey   "A Brief History of Abstinence," *Time*, March 2, 2009.

Melissa Fletcher   "Abstinence Can Be Taught Along
Stoeltje   with Contraception," *San Antonio Express-News*, May 5, 2012.

Amy Sullivan   "How to End the War Over Sex Ed," *Time*, April 6, 2009.

Index

A

Abortion
  education, 91, 104
  rates, 44, 47–48
  right to, 107
  sex education and, 89
Abstinence by Choice program, 17–18
Abstinence education programs
  background information on, 81–83
  behavioral change from, 12–20
  common characteristics of, 29–31
  costs associated with, 46–48
  criticism of, 80–81
  cultivation of ignorance, 48–49
  denigration through, 74–76
  as effective, 11–21, 83–85
  federal funding for, 50–58
  harm from, 28–29, 76–77
  inadequate evaluation of, 37–39
  as ineffective, 22–31, 42–49
  introduction, 7–10
  no benefit to, 24–26, 77–78
  no shame and guilt from, 79–86
  out of touch with reality, 23–24
  overview, 22–23, 32–33, 42–43, 72–73, 79–80
  personal viewpoint on, 73–74
  protection of youth, 11–12
  remarketing of, 31

  risk taking by adolescents and, 33–35
  sexual risks and, 39–41
  shame and guilt from, 72–78
  societal benefit of, 20–21
  state decisions in, 43–45
  teen pregnancy and, 32–41
Abstinence-only Intervention study, 12–13
Abstinence-only-until-marriage education
  characteristics of, 29–31
  federal funding for, 8, 10, 23, 27–28, 63
  as ineffective, 24–26, 98
  as isolating, 101
  religious conservatism of, 29
  support for, 22–23
Adolescent Family Life Act (AFLA), 8, 23, 25, 27, 33, 43
Adolescent risk taking, 33–35
Affordable Care Act, 107
African Americans, 62, 69
Alexander, Calah, 72–78, 81
American Academy of Pediatrics, 25
American Medical Association, 12
American Psychological Association, 25
American Social Hygiene Association, 7
Archives of Pediatrics and Adolescent Medicine (journal), 12
ASPIRE: Live Your Life. Be Free, 29, 30
Attempted suicide, 98
AVERT charity, 87–96